CHARTISM AND THE CHURCHES

Charles Seale-Hayne Library
University of Plymouth
(01752) 588 588
LibraryandITenquiries@plymouth.ac.uk

CHARTISM
AND THE CHURCHES

A STUDY IN DEMOCRACY

by

Harold Underwood Faulkner

FRANK CASS & CO. LTD.

1970

Published by
FRANK CASS AND COMPANY LIMITED
67 Great Russell Street, London WC1
by arrangement with Columbia University Press

This title was first published as Number 3,
Volume LXXIII, of
STUDIES IN HISTORY, ECONOMICS AND PUBLIC LAW,
edited by the Faculty of Political Science
of Columbia University

First edition	1916
New impression	1970

ISBN 0 7146 1308 8 ⌣

0054625

*Printed in Great Britain by Clarke, Doble & Brendon Ltd.
Plymouth and London*

PREFACE

THE real significance of the Chartist movement has only recently been realized. Its apparent sudden collapse under circumstances humiliating to its followers has enabled the average bourgeois historian to dismiss the whole subject with a few remarks emphasizing chiefly some humorous incidents of the closing scene. The influence of the movement in arousing the English proletariat to a class consciousness and in preparing them for their inevitable share in the political structure of English democracy has never been adequately appreciated, while the part taken by the Chartists and their leaders in the various reform movements of the time has been almost ignored. Outside of the interesting and straightforward history of Gammage, a prominent Chartist, most of the attention devoted to the subject has been by French and German scholars, the sum total of which, however, has been astonishingly small when the importance of Chartism is considered.

By the religious and political radical the idea that organized Christianity as represented in the churches has ordinarily been opposed to progress, especially scientific and political, has long been accepted as a truism. Ardent churchmen, on their side, aroused by the taunts of their opponents and under the spell of an expanding democracy and new conceptions of social justice, have in recent years endeavored to picture Christ as the first great reformer and his teachings as a platform advanced enough for the most radical. Realizing that a large element of truth underlies the arguments of both groups and with no intention to answer generally any of the questions involved, the author has thought it worth while to take some important movement in favor of democracy and examine as closely as the available sources permitted the attitude of the various churches toward it. Because of the slight attention heretofore given it and because of its unique position as the first distinctly proletariat agitation of modern times the Chartist movement has been chosen.

In the preparation of this essay the author is largely indebted to Professor James T. Shotwell, under whose direction the work was done and from whose criticisms the thesis has profited; to Professor Edwin R. A. Seligman, who put at his disposal the Chartist collection in his private library; to Professor William Walker Rockwell of Union Theological Seminary, who read the thesis and made numerous suggestions; and to his Father, Professor John Alfred Faulkner of Drew Theological Seminary.

H. U. F.

MADISON, N. J., *April 10, 1916.*

TABLE OF CONTENTS

CHAPTER I

ATTITUDE OF CHARTISM TOWARDS THE CHURCH

I. RELIGION OF THE WORKING CLASSES

The Reform Bill of 1832 was the first notable result of the Industrial Revolution upon the constitutional framework of the English Government. It increased the electorate and recognized the distribution of population in the awarding of representation. But the Reform Bill of 1832 was not a democratic measure. Although both the middle and lower classes had contributed to the struggle for its adoption only the former benefited from it. The lower bourgeoisie and proletariat, comprising the majority of the population, were still left without the vote, and to them the Reform Bill was to be but the first step toward an ultimate democracy.

When the smoke of the struggle cleared away, the great class still disfranchised discovered that not only had they reaped no benefit from the reform they had so largely helped to win, but that their lot under a reformed Parliament dominated by the doctrines of the Manchester School seemed to be worse than ever. The political discontent of the people was at last given voice in 1838 when the People's Charter was launched under the supervision of the London Working Men's Association. The demands of the People's Charter which formed the program of the Chartist movement were six in number and included manhood suffrage, annual parliaments, vote by ballot, abolition of property qualifica-

tion for seats in Parliament, payment of members of
Parliament and division of the country into equal electoral
districts.[1]

Although the manifestations of Chartism were political,
its causes were largely economic.[2] The unparalleled
social misery of the people[3] gave to the Chartist movement a stimulus which made it in a sense but a sequel to
the agitations for factory reform and in opposition to the
New Poor Law. The attainment of the Charter was
expected to usher in the social millennium. But the most
significant feature of Chartism was that it was the first
distinctive workingmen's movement of modern times,[4]
and the Charter contained both their ideal of political
justice and their hope of social amelioration.[5]

---

[1] Gammage, *History of the Chartist Movement*, new ed. (London,
1894), Appendix B, where the Charter is given.

[2] Rogers, *Six Centuries of Work and Wages*, 6th ed. (London, 1901),
p. 440; Walpole, *History of England*, rev. ed. (London, 1902-5), iv,
50; Carlyle, *Chartism*, chapter i; Rose, *Rise of Democracy* (London,
1897), pp. 129, 130; *Wisconsin Academy of Science, Arts and Letters*
(Madison, 1900), xii, 567.

[3] *Parliamentary Papers*.

[4] Engels, *Socialism, Utopian and Scientific* (London, 1892), Introduction, p. xxx.

[5] It is outside the field of the monograph to enter into a history of
the Chartist Movement. The leading studies covering it will be found
in the bibliography under the heading "General Works" under
"Chartism." The chief source is the remarkably interesting but
detailed running account of R. G. Gammage, a prominent participant
in the agitation, in his *History of the Chartist Movement, 1837—1854*
(London, new ed., 1894). Failure to consider the social and economic
phases of the movement is its chief weakness. Next in importance to
Gammage is Eduard Dolleans' *Le Chartisme*, 2 vols. (Paris 1912), strong
in its development of the social and political theories of the proletariat
but disappointing to the student for its lack of footnotes. Tildsley in
his *Die Entstehung und die ökonomischen Grundsätze der Chartistenbewegung* (Jena, 1898) deals intelligently with the economic back-
ground and Dierlamm (*Die Flugschriftenliteratur der Chartistenbeweg-*

In this first great struggle of the proletariat the question as to the attitude of organized Christianity, as represented by the Church of England and the dissenting bodies, early presented itself. Would these churches officially keep out of the struggle entirely or would they line up on one side or the other? With the vast political and spiritual power of the churches enlisted in the cause of democracy success was assured; without their co-operation the struggle would be infinitely harder. It is to an examination of the relationship of the English proletariat to the church during the years of the Chartist movement that the following pages are devoted.

In a study of the relationship between the Chartist movement and the church some attention should be given in the first place to the state of religion amongst the working class and the type of religion, if any, professed by them. The extraordinary increase of population following the English industrial revolution, an increase which in less than 150 years more than quadrupled the population of England alone,[1] could not fail but have its effect upon the religious life of the country. If the Established and Nonconformist churches were able approximately to take care of the population in 1750, the reverse was true seventy-five years later. Population, especially in the large towns which sprang up with astonishing rapidity[2] all over Great Britain, had long since

---

ung und ihr Widerhall in der öffentlichen Meinung, Leipzig, 1909) with the pamphlet literature and its effect. Carlyle's *Chartism* (1839) is merely an interpretation.

[1] The population of England in 1750 was about 6,467,000 ; in 1911 about 34,045,290.

[2] Weber, *Growth of Cities in the Nineteenth Century* (N. Y., 1899), p. 40 *et. seq.*

outgrown the antiquated machinery of the State Church.[1] Although the Church of England was taking on a new lease of life through the enthusiasm engendered by the Oxford movement, and because parliamentary investigations and Ecclesiastical Commissions had made it necessary, only a beginning had yet been made in reclaiming the lost multitude. In Leeds, a parish numbering 150,-000, the parish church had fifty communicants.[2] Nor had the Dissenters been able to take advantage of the opportunity; most of the sects by the second quarter of the 19th century represented almost entirely a middle-class constituency. Even the Wesleyan Methodist Church, which in early days had been preëminently the church of the manufacturing and mining poor and, but for its mode of government, might have earned the name of the Church of the Industrial Revolution, had by the beginning of the Chartist period also suffered the blight of respectability and had lost the confidence of the intelligent workingman because of the conservatism of its political policy, the Tory affiliations of its leading ministers and the undemocratic form of its government.

The support of the churches in England during this period was decidedly a middle-class affair. Observers of all types of religious thought recognized it. "What struck every cultivated foreigner who set up his residence in England", said Engels, who was a close observer, "was what he was bound to consider the religious bigotry and stupidity of the English respectable middle class."[3] Robertson as pastor in his new field at Brigh-

---

[1] *Parliamentary Reports of Ecclesiastical Commissions.* Perry, *A History of the English Church* (London, 1890), vol. iii, p. 260 *et seq.* Bloomfield, *A Memoir of Charles James Bloomfield* (London, 1863), vol. i, ch. ix.

[2] Perry, *op. cit.*, iii, 262.   [3] Engels, *Socialism*, p. xiv.

ton found only the middle class faithful.[1]   The *Church
of England Magazine* recognized fully this relation of
the middle class to English religion,[2] while Miall, the
most acute journalist of the Nonconformists, affirmed
that British Christianity was "essentially the Christianity
developed by a middle-class soil" and as such "fast de-
caying" and "void of efficiency."[3]

If a monopolization of religion by the bourgeoisie was
admitted, the lack on the part of the proletariat of a
formal religious affiliation with any sect was equally apparent and deplored by ministers of all denominations.
Says Mozley, one of the leaders of the High-Church
movement, "It may be truly said that the whole of
our manufacturing people, the whole of the poorer
classes in our towns, are alienated from the church.
Yet this does not express by any means the sum of their
misery.   An enormous proportion, three fourths or nine
tenths, are neither church people, nor of any other reli-

---

[1] Brooke, *Life and Letters of Frederick W. Robertson, M. A.* (New York, n. d,) p. 110.

[2] "Amidst the reports of infidelity reigning, either covertly or openly, over large bodies of men in Europe, it is satisfactory to find our middle classes so little affected by the plausibilities of false speculation.   Were they to lose their religious principles, the lower classes would soon break out into open infidelity, and then 'the beginning of the end' would be near.   Of this catastrophe there appears, at present, no sign ; though it is to be feared that false notions, and destructive ideas in morals, have infected numbers of the workmen in the towns and great factories.   Indeed, the middle classes are less likely to fall into such errors now than twenty years ago, when a dangerous spirit seemed brooding over the land, waiting for a signal to burst into fearful activity. It is in the religious activity of the middle classes that we must rely for the most effective checks to the evils arising from our highly artificial state of society, and from the spread of luxurious habits consequent upon the diffusion of wealth."   *The Church of England Magazine*, vol. xxiii, p. 20, (July 10, 1847).

[3] Miall, *Life of Edward Miall* (London, 1884), pp. 151, 152.

gion."[1] "An artizan with his wife and children," says
the same author, "are seldom seen anywhere; at church
never."[2] A workingman, who had given the subject
some thought, and who spoke from personal observation,
believed that a mechanic was " as seldom found in a religious assembly as a religious man in many of our workshops."[3] The causes for this alienation are not difficult
to ascertain. Christianity was "widely and truly believed to be as a whole opposed to the social aspirations
of the nation," and nothing could save it from the
"charge of being obstructive and reactionary."[4] The
workingmen turned disgustedly away from an Establishment which sought to perpetuate in the government
abuses only too apparent, and from the Dissenters, who,
after they had carried the Reform Bill of 1832, had, as
the workingmen believed, betrayed them.

To take the place of religious enthusiasm the workingmen found an outlet for their feelings in "reforming
clubs, Chartist gatherings, trades unions, and political
debating circles."[5] As regards religion the reaction
from the worn-out evangelicalism of the period developed itself along two lines. The first of these was infidelity. Modern free thought, launched by Herbert of
Cherbury and Hobbes, and taken up enthusiastically on
the Continent, now returned to the land of its birth, but-
tressed with all the learning of the rapidly developing
sciences. But whereas in its early days it was the play-

[1] *British Critic*, vol. 28, p. 346 (1840).
[2] *Ibid.*, p. 337.
[3] *The Literature of the Working Men*, vol. i, Apr. 1850, p. 5; also
vide *The Champion*, vol. i, p. 156 *et. seq.*
[4] Hall, *The Social Meaning of Modern Religious Movements in Eng-
and* (N. Y., 1900), p. 162.
[5] *Ibid.*, p. 168.

thing of aristocrats it now became the accepted creed of thousands of workingmen. "In order to find people who dared to use their own intellectual faculties with regard to religious matters," said Engels, "you had to go amongst the uneducated, the 'great unwashed', as they were called, the working people, especially the Owenite Socialists."[1] Kingsley was no less dogmatic. "The devil has got the best long ago," he complained, for "the cream and pith of working intellect is almost exclusively self-educated, and therefore, also infidel!"[2] Disraeli describes St. Lys, his ideal clergyman, as a vicar "who came among a hundred thousand heathen to preach the word of God."[3] This spread of infidelity was naturally distressing to the churchmen,[4] and it was a desire to win the workingman back to Christianity chiefly that moved Maurice and Kingsley to their philanthropic efforts for the poor of London.

The growth of infidelity was accentuated by the influence of the socialistic movement, which, up to that time in consequence of the well-known views of Owen, had been largely tinged with unbelief. The fact that many of the Chartist leaders and great hosts of their followers were both socialists and infidels gave a handle to the continued accusations of their enemies. Such Chartist leaders as Hetherington, Watson, Carlile, Walter Cooper and Holyoake were actively associated with one or more of the numerous infidel papers which usually also advocated socialism and incidentally Chartism as the most

[1] Engels, *Socialism*, p. xiv.

[2] *Charles Kingsley: His Letters and Memories of His Life*, ed. by *His Wife*, 10th ed. (London, 1878), pp. 234, 248; *Alton Locke*, p. 275.

[3] Disraeli, *Sybil*, p. 125.

[4] *Church of England Magazine*, xxiii, 20; *Christian Guardian*, 1847, p. 325; *Methodist Minutes*, ix, 115, 403.

practical means at hand for the inaugurating of the new social order,[1] while Thomas Cooper and others were active in the propaganda of David Friedrich Strauss, extremely popular in England among certain classes after the publication of "*Leben Jesu.*"[2] The works of Paine, Holyoake and other religious radicals were regularly advertised in many of the leading Chartist journals, including *The Northern Star*. The Englishmen of the upper and middle classes had already learned from French history to associate political radicalism with infidelity, and now the development in England seemed only to prove an inalienable connection between the two. Such phrases as "infidel democracy,"[3] "sedition and blasphemy,"[4] etc., came soon almost unconsciously to be part of the intellectual equipment of these two classes. "Republicans, Infidels, Sabbath-breakers and Blasphemers, who are, unhappily, a curse to themselves, a curse to their Fellow-Countrymen, and a curse to the land that owns them,"[5] is one description of the Chartists, and of by no means an exceptional type. The charge of infidelity naturally took its place as a leading stock argument against Chartism and was continually held up before the eyes of the horrified bourgeoisie in sermons, pamphlets and speeches to such an extent that the two were, in the minds of many, synonymous.

[1] The growth of the infidel press in England during this period is remarkable. It included such papers as, "*The Movement,*" edited by Holyoake and Ryall; "*The Reasoner: and Herald of Progress,*" backed by many leading Chartists; "*The Union,*" edited by G. A. Fleming; "*The Oracle of Reason,*" edited by Charles Southworth and Thomas Paterson; "*The Model Republic*" and "*Cooper's Journal.*"

[2] Translated by George Eliot, 1846.

[3] *Wesleyan Meth. Mag.*, Feb. 1838, vol. xvii, p. 153.

[4] *The People*, i, 333.

[5] *The Real Chartist*, by C. L., 4 ed. (London, 1848) p. 13.

The Chartists of course resented this,[1] and justly. for their ranks included many who, although having no connection or interest in the church, could still be designated as Christians.

The second reaction against the Christianity of the time as exemplified in the churches assumed a form far less violent than infidelity. It took the form of a feeling of either indifference or absolute hostility to the church and ecclesiasticism although coupled with loyalty to the tenets of Christianity. The group of persons actuated by this feeling undoubtedly far outnumbered either the infidels or the active church members.[2] The feeling of many was much like that which Solly puts in the mouth of his Chartist working man who says:

None of us had any great love for " the cloth." Not that we had any bad feelings towards them, but I believe we mostly thought the whole Church Establishment was a matter of money, and that all clergymen did and said their doings and sayings merely to get paid. So that we had rather a feeling of contempt for them because we thought them so uncommonly like hypocrites. The same with regard to religion generally. There was very little real enmity against it, as far as I could see, among workingmen. We only thought it a humbug, and not worth a sensible man's troubling his head about.[3]

The characterization of Solly is accurate in all but one respect. To the leaders, and, it is fair to infer, a majority of their followers, this attitude seemed too passive. They were bitterly opposed to the State Church and to the interpretation of Christianity which actuated all of the denominations, and waged a strenuous campaign in be-

---

[1] *The Republican*, p. 73 *et seq.*

[2] *Ibid.*, p. 76.

[3] Solly, *James Woodford* (London, 1881), i, 214.

half of their views. The Chartists had both a distinct conception of their own as to what Christianity was and a definite program of church reform.

One student of the movement believes that the majority of Chartists belonged to the State Church.[1] But to infer, as he does, that such is the case because they attended the parish church on occasion is erroneous. One clergyman upon such a visit went so far as to tell them that their coming to a church was something out of the ordinary.[2] It seems nearer the truth to say that the Chartists, while a majority were decided believers in Christianity, were indifferent toward all the churches.

The Chartist leaders were drawn from all denominations. Among the infidels were numbered Hetherington, Watson, Carlile, Holyoake and Walter Cooper. The Established Church of England contributed Charles Westerton, Dr. Arthur S. Wade and Rev. Thomas Spencer; the Established Church of Scotland, Rev. Patrick Brewster; and the Secessionists, Dr. John Ritchie. Giles was a Baptist, Miall a Congregationalist, O'Malley a Catholic. Sturge and Pierce were Quakers. Rev. J. R. Stephens started as a Methodist minister, was expelled for his activities in promoting the separation of Church and State,[3] and continued as pastor of three chapels near Ashley built by the workingmen there,[4] 800 of the members of his circuit having seceded with him. Thomas Cooper as a young man was a Methodist local preacher. During the Chartist period he drifted to infidelity, but eventually returned to Christianity and be-

---

[1] Dierlamm, *Die Flugschriftenliteratur der Chartistenbewegung und ihr Widerhall in der öffentlichen Meinung* (Leipzig, 1909), p. 60.

[2] *Dr. Whittaker's Sermon to the Chartists*, p. 14.

[3] Smith, *History of Methodism*, bk. viii, ch. ii.

[4] Gammage, *History of the Chartist Movement*, p. 56.

came a minister of the Baptists.[1] Joseph Barker, born and educated a Wesleyan Methodist, forsook that church for the Methodist New Connexion, from which he was expelled on doctrinal grounds.[2] He became a Unitarian, later a deist, but finally he too returned to Christianity. Lovett's mother was a Methodist, while he himself was for a short while a Bryanite (Methodist Bible Christian).[3] A defender of Christianity,[4] he belonged to no church. When asked by the chaplain, on his admission to prison, what was his religion, he answered that he " was of that religion which Christ taught, and which very few in authority practice " if he might judge from their conduct.[5] O'Neill in his later life became a Baptist minister[6] as did Vince. Vincent, while not a member, was a frequent attendant in Quaker meetings and active in their work.[7] Henry Solly and W. J. Fox were both prominent Chartists and leading Unitarian ministers.

II CHARTISM AND CHRISTIANITY

A. THE CHARTIST INTERPRETATION OF CHRISTIANITY

Although the English Chartist was a stranger to the church, he was, as a rule, familiar with the teachings of Christ and soon came to entertain some definite ideas in regard to Christianity. He reduced it to a formula simple but practical. He emphasized only the social aspect,

[1] Cooper, *Life of Thomas Cooper*, 2nd ed, (London, 1872), pp. 81, 82.

[2] *New History of Methodism* (London, 1909), i, 525.

[3] Lovett, *Life and Struggles of William Lovett in His Pursuit of Bread, Knowledge, and Freedom* (London, 1876), pp. 7, 22.

[4] *Ibid.*, p. 35.

[5] *Ibid.*, p. 229.

[6] Gammage, *op. cit.* p. 402.

[7] *Dict. of Nat. Biog.*, lviii, p. 359.

Christianity in his mind being comprised largely in
Matthew xxii, 39; xxv, and similar sections. These he
took seriously. "If one thing is more certain than
another," said one, "it is this, that it is the duty of
Christians to labour for the welfare of their fellow-
men."¹ The typical Chartist viewpoint was similar to
that of Lovett, who said he had come "to look upon
practical Christianity as a union for the promotion of
loving kindness and good deeds to one another, and not
a thing of form for idlers to profit by, who in their
miserable interpretation of it too often cause men to
neglect the improvement of the present in their aspirations of the future."²

If Christianity could be reduced to a matter of the
Golden Rule³ what was the use of forms and ceremonies,
of priests and masses? Why worry about creeds when
the commands for action were so plain? It was not
more churches that England needed, they thought, but
an "increase of pure, practical and undefiled religion,"
for "church going is but a means to an end."⁴ What is
necessary to regenerate the world, says Alton Locke,
"is not more of any system good or bad, but simply
more of the Spirit of God."⁵ Consequently when the
Chartists essayed themselves to put their hands to the
task of organizing and running a church, they eliminated
creeds, as such, although retaining baptism and the
Lord's Supper, and put the entire emphasis upon good
works.⁶

¹ *The People*, pp. 19, 20.
² Lovett, *Life and Struggles*, p. 35.
³ *Chartist Circular*, p. 5.
⁴ *Livesey's Moral Reformer*, p. 133.
⁵ P. 105.
⁶ *Vide infra*, p. 42 *et seq.*

The more they studied the words of Christ, the more they were struck with the illogicality of the situation as it existed.   The Established Church with its vast wealth, highly paid functionaries and elaborate ceremonial appeared to them the very antithesis of Christianity; while the Dissenters, engrossed in endless differences over doctrine and church government, and generally aloof to the needs of social amelioration at their doors, seemed equally astray.   How any professing Christian could remain indifferent to the miserable condition prevalent among the manufacturing and agricultural poor was to the Chartist a mystery.   But not only was the church indifferent to their state but it was accused of joining hands "with bloodthirsty and deceitful men to render their misery complete and irremediable."[1]

What the Chartists wanted to see on the part of professing Christians was some practical demonstrations of the social teachings of Christ which should take the form of an effort to improve their lot.   Nor was it charity they demanded so much as justice.[2]   Christ and Christianity to them meant the "lifting of heavy burthens and bringing them freedom and justice as well as soup-tickets and tracts."[3]

Once granted that the mission of Christianity was to bring to them freedom and social justice, the only question remaining to be settled was how this object could be best promoted.   The English workingman had decided that the only hope lay in the People's Charter. The natural sequence was that Chartism was therefore divine and ordained of God.[4]   "Study the New Testa-

---

[1] Stephens, *Sermon on Kennington Common* (London, 1839), p. 20.

[2] Solly, *James Woodford*, i, 213.

[3] *Ibid.*, i, 237, 238.

[4] *Chartist Circular*, preface, iv; pp. 1, 5, 9, 32, 197.

ment—it contains the elements of Chartism," exhorted one paper.[1] The conception of the connection between the question of the franchise and Christianity not only took strong hold of the workingman, but it was one influence, if not the chief one, in winning for the Chartists what little aid they received from the middle classes. It was the actuating motive of the so-called "political preachers," like Stephens, Spencer and Parsons and furnished the ordinary theme for the sermons of the Christian Chartist Churches. Joseph Sturge, the leader of the Complete Suffrage movement, the single concerted middle-class effort in behalf of the Charter, was brought to take an active part through this influence. "It is a distinguishing and beautiful feature of Christianity," said he, "that it leads us to recognize every country as our country, and every man as our brother ; and as there is no moral degradation so awful, no physical misery so great as that inflicted by personal slavery, I have felt it my duty to labour for its universal extinction."[2] "Nothing is more certain," says his biographer, "than that what was called the Chartism of Joseph Sturge sprung directly from his Christianity."[3] It was also the keynote of the work of Edward Miall in his editorials on universal suffrage. The address of the " *Council of the National Complete Suffrage Association to Political Reformers of all Shades of Opinion,*" calling upon them in September, 1842, to elect representatives to a convention, is remarkable in that it acts under " that great Christian obligation" which " calls upon all men to assist in freeing their brethren from the powers of the op-

---

[1] *Chartist Circular*, p. 222.

[2] Richard, *Memoirs of Joseph Sturge* (London, 1864), p. 299.

[3] *Ibid.*, p. 325.

pression " and addresses them as "men and Christians," desiring not to arouse their passions but simply to "awake the nobler feelings of justice, humanity and Christian duty"[1]

But the Chartists approached the fact that universal suffrage was based "on the revealed word of God"[2] from still another angle. They attempted to prove the "divine origin of liberty" from the laws of nature as ordained by God, and sought to prove from the Scriptures that "a simple democracy was the only order of government" instituted by God.[3] As expressed on one of their banners: "Every man is born free: God has given to all men equal rights and equal liberties."[4]

Neither of these conceptions was original. The belief in the divine origin of liberty was much older than Chartism, while the idea of finding a basis for political beliefs in Christianity of course was not confined to the Chartists. Quotations from the Bible furnished to their opponents some strong weapons.

B. CHRISTIANITY AND POLITICS

Having convinced themselves that democracy was ordained of God, and that loving one's neighbors as oneself was vitally connected with political justice, it seemed to the Chartist that the professing Christian was in duty bound to do his utmost to advance his cause. If it was the duty of Christian laymen to aid in the political emancipation of the proletariat, in a how much greater degree was it the business of their leaders, the clergy and pastors, the recognized expounders of the truths of Christianity!

[1] Lovett, *Life and Struggles*, p. 276, *et. seq.*
[2] *Chartist Circular*, p. 9.	[3] *Ibid.*, p. 1.
[4] Dolleans, *Le Chartisme* (Paris, 1912), ii, 466.

But this view again brought them into direct antagonism with the church. The simple process of reasoning which carried the Chartists to their conclusion as to the duty of a Christian had no weight with the latter in regard to political matters. A peculiar and widely held doctrine had taken hold of early nineteenth-century Christianity in England to the effect that it was "wrong for a Christian to meddle in political matters."[1] To concern oneself with politics was almost sure to result in contamination and was always fraught with danger to the spiritual welfare of the participant.[2] All of the denominations were particularly careful to disavow any political affiliation and he who was least concerned with the "affairs of this world" was considered the most saintly and worthy of emulation. To be indifferent to political interests was considered a mark of piety.

Although this feeling that there was something antagonistic between Christianity and politics was prevalent in all of the churches, it found its greatest exponents among the Wesleyan Methodists.[3] "It is no business of ours as 'men of God' who have dedicated ourselves to a kingdom which 'is not of this world,'" affirmed the Conference of 1836, "to be very eager or prominent in drawing out these great principles to what we deem right political conclusions."[4] For a Methodist minister to engage in political controversy was to act "contrary to his peculiar calling and solemn engagements."[5] Even the Congregationalists, unencumbered, as were the Meth-

---

[1] *Reformer's Almanac*, p. 284.

[2] *Epistles from the Yedrly Meetings of Friends*, ii, 303, 332.

[3] Lovett, *Life and Struggles*, p. 244 ; Davison, *Life of the Venerable William Clowes* (London, 1854), p. 241.

[4] *Minutes*, viii, 105. See also pp. 237, 242 ; x, 260.

[5] *Minutes*, ii, 185.

odists, by conservative traditions, hastened in 1841 to disclaim any possible political affiliation or interest, after a session of the Congregationalist Union devoted largely to a discussion of this subject,[1] and the editor of the Congregationalist asserted that as regards the redress of civil grievances "Christian ministers have no especial concern, and Christian churches and congregations, as such, no proper concern at all."[2] The maintenance of Christian virtues, says the Yearly Conference of Friends, "is much endangered by yielding to political excitement."[3]

Deeply grounded as was the feeling that the effect of politics was detrimental to religion, it was still not so strong but that most of the churches were willing to be contaminated a bit when their interests were seen to be endangered. The Established Church worked effectually through their representatives in the House of Lords and other innumerable avenues; the Methodists maintained after 1803 a "Committee of Privileges," whose duty it was to look after those matters pertaining to the civil rights of their people, while after 1832 the dissenting churches had many friends in the Lower House. The political power of the Dissenters was never shown more effectively than in 1843 when they successfully opposed the educational clause in Lord Graham's Factory Bill. By the time of the Chartist period, however, the objection to active political participation on the part of the clergy was beginning to break down. The Anti-Corn Law League succeeded in interesting several hundred ministers in their cause and in holding a conference of ministers of religion in Manchester on behalf of cheap

[1] Waddington, *Congregational History 1800–1850* (London, 1878), p. 553.

[2] *Ibid.*, p. 573.

[3] *Epistle From the Yearly Meetings of Friends*, ii, 303.

grain. Ministers of all denominations participated, including even one each from the Established Church of Scotland and the Wesleyan Methodists.[1]

The viewpoint of the churches that political matters were not to be compared in importance to the things immediately pertaining to salvation[2] was not shared by the Chartists. Christianity was to them above all practical, something that must be carried into every walk of life. Furthermore there was no possibility of divorcing it from political science. Thus Rev. William Hill, editor of the *Northern Star*, in a lecture said:

Politics, then, is the science of human government. It is a science that teaches men their rights, and the best way of exercising them, and, digging deep into the foundation of this science, it may be considered as an essential but much neglected branch of Christian ethics. We are commanded, for example, to love our neighbors as ourselves; this has usually been considered as applying to our duty so far as the exercise of charity is concerned; but this command is universal in its application, whether as friend, Christian or citizen. A man may be devout as a Christian, faithful as a friend, but if as a citizen he claims rights for himself he refuses to confer upon others, he fails to fulfill the precept of Christ; taking this view of politics what an important view does it give this subject, compared with the narrow, partizan ideas usually associated with the term.[3]

But the typical Chartist went through the evolution of mind similar to that described by the Rev. Joseph Barker who said:

[1] Prentice, *History of the Anti-Corn Law League* (London, 1835), vol. i, pp. 233 *et seq.*

[2] *Meth. Minutes*, viii, 96.

[3] *The Life Boat*, vol. i, no. 4.

Formerly I thought it wrong for a Christian to meddle in political matters. Formerly I thought it the duty of Christians to unite themselves together in churches, to shut themselves out from the world, to constitute themselves a little exclusive world, and to confine their labours to the government of their little kingdom and to the increase of the numbers of its subjects. I now think differently. I have no faith in church organizations. I believe it my duty to be a man ; to live and move in the world at large ; to battle with evil wherever I see it, and to aim at the annihilation af all corrupt institutions and at the establishment of all good, and generous, and useful institutions in their places.[1]

The most striking attempt of the Chartists to associate politics and religion was in the Christian Chartist Churches, where Christianity and radical politics were brought together and believed to be inseparable.[2]   But it was not confined to these. Solly tells of a friend of his, a Chartist lecturer by the name of Clarke, who on his tours alternated his political lectures with sermons.[3]

It was the attempt to associate Christianity with practical politics that was chiefly responsible for the great popularity of the few preachers who were willing to brave the storm of public abuse and calumny which was associated with the term " political preacher." The Rev. J. R. Stephens was the most famous of this class. The effect of his discourses upon the multitudes who, " after a week of toil would stand for hours, regardless of comfort and health, while the rain fell in torrents—to hear the exhortations fall from his lips "[4]—can hardly be

---

[1] *Reformer's Almanac*, p. 284.

[2] *Vide infra*, p. 42 *et seq.*

[3] Solly, *These Eighty Years* (London, 1893), vol. i, p. 385.

[4] Stephens, *Sermon Preached on Shepherd and Shepherdess Fields* (1839), introduction.

imagined. Gifted with great eloquence, his intense bitterness toward the factory system and the New Poor Law often led him into extravagant statements of the most inflammatory kind,[1] which, printed in the *Northern Star* and distributed in pamphlet form, gave to him an influence upon the Chartist movement in its early stages hardly exceeded by O'Connor himself. Another gifted preacher of this class was Eustace Giles, a prominent Baptist, who was spoken of as "one of the pioneers who believed that it is often needful to be political in order to give expression to one's religious convictions."[2] The Rev. Thomas Spencer, Church of England clergyman, and the Rev. Henry Solly, Unitarian, both pamphleteers and preachers, the Rev. Joseph Barker and Rev. William Hill, editors and lecturers, were other political preachers who distinguished themselves in the Chartist movement. Many more, including such names as Edward Miall and James Scholefield, could be added to the list. The "political preacher," in the modern sense of the term, first came into prominence in the agitations incidental to the Anti-Corn Law and Chartist movements.

III. ATTITUDE OF THE CHARTISTS TOWARD THE CHURCH AND CLERGY

The bitterness of the Chartists towards the churches and clergy, especially those of the State Church, approached almost of unanimity. The periodical and pamphlet literature and the reported speeches are full of the severest condemnation. The Established Church is described as "ungodly" and "plundering,"[3] as "villainous,"[4] as "old

---

[1] Gammage, *op. cit.*, p. 55 *et seq.*

[2] Carlile, *Story of the English Baptists* (London, 1905), p. 231.

[3] *Reformer's Almanac*, p. 19.   [4] *Reformer's Companion*, p. 19.

mother hypocrisy," " hatch houses of fraud and hypocrisy "
and " this country's neglected curse," [1] as a " superstitious
Old Hog," " an administration of Atheism " and " a system
of vile priestcraft, encouraged by the aristocracy, for the
plunder of the church revenues, and for the keeping of the
people in a state of ignorance and suitable slavery and
debasement," [2] as " the most corrupt and oppressive institution in Europe," [3] and as " one of the greatest bulwarks of despotism, and barriers of freedom in the annals
of our country," whose " course has been one of mischief,
cruelty and plunder." [4]   The clergy are characterized by
The People as " reckless perjured liars," " vile infernal
cheats," " ministers of the Devil," " blasphemers of God,"
" teachers of fables," " preachers of licentiousness," " anti-
Christs." [5]   McDouall refers to them as "infidels," "proud,"
" rapacious," " cruel," " ambitious," " fraudulent," and
" hypocritical." [6]   The *Reformer's Companion* calls them
" vile," [7] and the *Weekly Adviser* "narrow souled, ignorant,
unreasoning," and " a positive disgrace to English civilization, and the bitterest enemies of the people." [8]   *The
National* denounces them as " a sable society of gentlemen,
wearing broad hats and deep garments; who possess a great
part of the wealth and power in the world, and would have
all, as a reward for keeping mankind in decent ignorance
and bondage." [9]

[1] *McDouall's Chartist and Republican Journal*, p. 34.

[2] Carlile, *An Address to that Portion of the People of Great Britain
and Ireland calling Themselves Reformers, on the Political Excitement
of the Present Time*, p. 6.

[3] Leach, *The Workingman's Argument in Favor of the Charter*, p. 8.

[4] *Evenings with the People*, p. 2.   [5] *The People*, p. 10.

[6] *McDouall's Chartist and Republican Journal*, p. 149. *Vide* also *Reformer's Companion*, p. 19, and *Reformer's Almanac*, p. 19.

[7] *Reformer's Companion*, p. 191.

[8] *Weekly Adviser and Artizan's Companion*, p. 161.

[9] *The National*, p. 241.

Although the dissenting churches were not the recipients of such wholesale and unqualified abuse as was the State Church they did not wholly escape. The Wesleyan Methodists were in particularly bad favor among reformers. It was a simple matter for the radicals of that period to account for the enmity of the Establishment but the fact that the Wesleyan Methodists, whose constituency was largely amongst the poorer classes, could steadfastly set their faces against all political reform was incomprehensible and called down the severest censure upon their administration and attitude. Gammage asserts " that if there is a body of men in England who are in the service and uphold the principles of despotism, that body is the Wesleyan Conference ",[1] which he describes as a " solemn hypocritical conclave." [2] Barker characterized the " Methodist preachers as a body " as " afraid of liberty in all its forms " [3] and the denomination as doing much harm by upholding the tyranny of the national government and " prejudicing its members against Reformers; against the advocates of truth and righteousness; and by representing the friends of truth, of justice, and of liberty, as infidels and anarchists." [4]   Ebenezer Elliott, who never got over the fact that the Wesleyan Methodists were the only dissenting church which would not participate actively in the Anti-Corn Law agitation, celebrated their degeneracy in rhyme.[5]

[1] Gammage, *op. cit.*, pp. 55, 56.   [2] *Ibid.*, p. 56.
[3] *The People*, vol. ii, p. 33.
[4] *Reformer's Almanac*, p. 370.
[5] " Ask ye if I, of Wesley's followers one,
            Abjure the home where Wesleyans bend the knee?
        I do—because the spirit thence is gone;
            And truth, and faith, and grace are not, with me,
            The Hundred Popes of England's Jesuitry."
                The Ranters, vol. i, p. 145 of the 1830 ed. of his poems.

The indictment formulated by the Chartists against the English clergy was a formidable one. They were, in the first place, accused of neglect of duty, especially as regards their poorer parishioners.

We ask [said Stephens], whether the ministers of religion in these times of savage and relentless, of stiffnecked and audacious tyranny, have faithfully discharged the duties of their holy office? They have not. Instead of pleading the cause of the poor, they have joined the league against them. They have shared in the murderous assault and are dividing the spoil.[1]

It was maintained, in the second place, that the clergy neither taught the true Christianity nor exemplified it in their lives. O'Brien found " almost every doctrine of holy writ falsified " in their lives [2] while Carlile held that the church had " no authority for (its) present proceedings in the Bible." [3]   Stephens affirmed that if the Gospel were " fairly, impartially, divinely preached in England for seven days, the end of the seventh day would behold the end of social tyranny as it afflicts the people." [4]   Thirdly, the Chartists found the church and clergy hostile to reform and accused them of deliberately using their influence to retard progress and to keep the people in ignorance and superstition.

Spencer, himself a Church of England clergyman, admitted that " all who advocate the removal of abuses are described as enemies of the church " and all political reformers, " find-

---

[1] *The People's Magazine*, p. 180, and vol. ii, p. 27. *Vide* also, Stephens, *Sermon on Kennington Common*, p. 25; *Is There One Law for the Rich and One for the Poor*, by a Workingman; *McDouall's Chartist and Republican Journal*, p. 149.

[2] *McDouall's Chartist and Republican Journal*, p. 149.

[3] Carlile, *Address*, p. 6.

[4] Stephens, *Sermon Preached on Shepherd and Shepherdess Field*, p. 6.

ing the church standing in the way of every reform, desire
its removal in order that they may obtain an extension of
the suffrage and a reformed Parliament, equitable taxation
and just laws." [1]

You uniformly prostitute religion to the maintenance of civil
tyranny [said O'Brien in a letter to the Established Church
parsons, and continued:] They (the people) see that holy writ
abounds from one end of the volume to the other in denunciation against usury and tyranny, and in threats of divine vengeance against oppressors of all kinds, and yet in the teeth of
these denunciations and solemn menaces, they behold you em-
ploying all the power of your craft to bolster up the system.[2]

To maintain, as the Chartists did, that the clergy of
England were remiss in their duty, that they did not preach
Christianity, and that they were the upholders of tyranny
was all very well, but the argument remained in the realm
of uncertainty. On these points it was possible to have
an honest difference of opinion. But the Chartists were
equipped with a more telling and practical criticism. The
unequal distribution of wealth in the Established Church,
resulting in extraordinarily large incomes for the bishops
and higher dignitaries and many sinecures, had been for
years the constant theme of radical reformers.[3] Although
the reforms of 6 and 7 William IV, Chapter 77, had done
something to remedy the evils,[4] the latter were still suffi-
ciently glaring, and the Chartist periodicals never wearied
of expatiating upon the princely incomes of the " servants
of him who ' had not where to lay his head.' " [5]   " For our-

---

[1] Spencer, *The Pillars of the Church of England*, p. ii.
[2] *McDouall's Chartist and Republican Journal*, p. 149.
[3] Stoughton, *Religion in England* (London, 1881-4), vol. viii, chap. i.
[4] Perry, *History of the English Church*, 3d Period, p. 233.
[5] *The People*, p. 21.

selves," says the *Weekly Adviser,* after giving a list of the bishops and their salaries, " we have no hesitation in saying that a highway robber is more worthy of honour than any one of the consecrated hypocrites named." [1]   The estimated nine million pounds income per annum [2] of the Established Church was looked upon as little less than robbery and the Church was called by one paper, " The Pious Pickpocket." [3] "Are you not paying too much for your whistle? " asks another.[4]   A third paper, after stating that a bishop in a twelvemonth did but a tithe of the duties, judged on a basis of utility, done in a single day by the humblest workman in its own office, cries: " How long is all this to last? " [5]

IV. PROGRAM OF THE CHARTISTS IN RESPECT TO THE CHURCH

The attitude of the Chartists towards the church early crystallized into a more or less definite program.   There must be, first of all, an absolute separation of church and state. On this point there was scarcely a difference of opinion. Cooper, Lovett, Barker, O'Brien and practically all the rest of the leaders believed this thoroughly.   Among the Chartist papers which strongly advocated it are to be numbered, *The Weekly Adviser,* [6] *The Model Republic, Power of Pence, The People,* [7] *The Reformer,* [8] *The Divinearian, The English Republic,* [9] *Cooper's Journal,* [10] *Bronterre's National*

[1] June 10, 1852, p. 12.
[2] Lovett, *op. cit.,* p. 266.
[3] *The Weekly Adviser,* June 10, 1852, p. 12.
[4] *The Model Republic,* p. 64.
[5] *Power of Pence,* p. 49 (Dec. 2, 1848).
[6] *The Weekly Adviser,* p. 2.
[7] *The People,* p. 1.
[8] *The Reformer,* p. 1.
[9] *The English Republic,* p. 86.
[10] *Cooper's Journal,* p. 143.

Reformer,[1] *McDouall's Chartist and Republican Journal*
and many more, including *The Non-conformist.*[2] In conjunction with the severance of church and state the voluntary
principle must be introduced. "If the preacher must be paid,"
said Ernest Jones, "let him be paid what he is worth and
if he is worthless let him not be paid at all."[3] Voluntaryism should be accompanied by the abolition of the hated
church tithes, the idea of supporting a church whose doctrines they detested being especially abhorrent to the Chartists.[4] An absolute cessation of persecution with complete
toleration on the part of the government to all religious
sects was of course an integral part of all reform.[5]

The radical doctrines with respect to church reform,
which had been informally set forth many times,[6] were
finally given official sanction at the Convention of 1851,
when the following propositions were recommended:

1st.   Complete separation of church and state.

2nd.   All church temporalities to be declared national property, except such individual endowments as have been voluntarily and legally made.

All ecclesiastical buildings, the cost of which can be clearly
shown to have been defrayed from national funds, to belong to
the state. The persuasion now using these edifices to continue
in the enjoyment of them on equitable conditions.

3rd.   Tithes and church rates to be abolished.

---

[1] *Bronterre's National Reformer*, Sat., Jan. 15, 1837, p. 61.

[2] Miall, *Life of Edward Miall,* pp. 50 *et seq.*

[3] *Evenings with the People*, p. 28.

[4] *The Radical Reformers of England, Scotland and Wales to the
Irish People,* p. 2 (written by Lovett); also *The Weekly Adviser,* p. 2.

[5] Lovett, *Life and Struggles,* p. 320; also *The People's Charter by the
Author of The Reformer Catechised, etc.,* pp. 47, 48.

[6] For the best examples, see *ibid.,* pp. 47, 48, and *Bronterre's National
Reformer* for Sat., Jan. 15, 1837, p. 11.

4th. The state not to interfere with the national policy of any church.   All ecclesiastics to be appointed in any way their respective congregations think fit, and to be paid voluntarily by the congregations that employ their services.

5th. Ecclesiastical licences for the purpose of education unnecessary.[1]

V. VISITS TO THE CHURCHES

The protests of the Chartists against the attitude of the Established, and other churches were not confined to press or platform denunciation.   During the severe government prosecutions of 1839, when the Chartists found their right of public meeting infringed upon, they adopted the method of assembling on the Sabbath and attending the parish churches in a body for the double purpose of displaying their numbers [2] and of registering their dissatisfaction at the position assumed by the church.

In the midsummer of 1839 this procedure seems to have been especially popular.   In July of that year the Chartists at Newcastle " went in a body and filled St. Nicholas church during divine service, to the great annoyance of the regular attendance." [3]   On August 4th a body " estimated at 1,500 formed in procession and made their way to Stockport church; and immediately on the doors being opened, took complete possession of the edifice." [4] On the same day about 4,000 visited the church at Blackburn.[5]   The next Sunday at Bolton, " Having met in the New Marketplace, to the number of 3,000 or 4,000, at an early hour, they proceeded at half-past nine o'clock, in

---

[1] *Notes to the People*, vol. i, p. 133; Gammage, *op. cit.*, p. 371.

[2] Gammage, *op. cit.*, p. 153.

[3] *Ibid.*, p. 149.

[4] *Gentleman's Magazine*, vol. xii, p. 301.

[5] *A Sermon Preached at the Parish Church, Blackburn, Sunday, August 4th, 1839*, by the Rev. J. W. Whittaker, D. D., p. 13.

processional order, six abreast, and in a few minutes completely filled the church."[1]   About 500 men in the same way on that day went to St. Paul's Cathedral.[2]   On August 18th Pastor Close preached to the Chartists at Cheltenham[3] and on the next Sunday addressed the Female Chartists of the same place.[4]   On November 17th Rev. Evan Jenkins of Dowlais received a similar visit.   These visits were only a few of the actual number made; for the idea, as Disraeli said, had much affected the imagination of the multitude.[5]

The Chartists usually gave previous intimation to the clergy of their intention,[6] recommending them to preach from such texts as, " The husband-man that laboureth shall be the first partaker of the fruits," " He who will not work shall not eat," etc.[7]   The clergy however

---

[1] *Gentleman's Magazine*, vol. xii, p. 301.   [2] *Ibid.*

[3] Close, *A Sermon Addressed to the Chartists of Cheltenham.*

[4] Close, *A Sermon Addressed to the Female Chartists of Cheltenham.* Rev. Francis Close was one of the leading Evangelicals of that period. An historian of that party, in speaking of him, says: " The latter ranked with Stowell and McNeile as one of the orators of the party, and he ruled Cheltenham from his pulpit throne to such an extent that the wits described it as ' a Close borough '. He fought the local magistrates and stopped the races. No meeting could be held without his permission. ' He was the pope of Cheltenham,' said *The Times*, ' with pontifical prerogatives from which the temporal had not been severed. In the bosoms of hundreds and thousands of householders his social decrees were accepted without the thought of the possibility of opposition. If a popular preacher is to be presented with a scepter, it may be admitted that none could have held it more judiciously or more uprightly '." Balleine, G. R., *A History of the Evangelical Party* (London, 1908), p. 205. The two sermons mentioned here were both strong denunciations of Chartism and called forth in reply two editorial leaders in the *Chartist Circular*. *Vide* vol. i, pp. 193, 205.

[5] Disraeli, *Sybil*, p. 375.

[6] Gammage, *op. cit.*, p. 153; Whittaker, *op. cit.*, p. 13; Close, *Female Chartists*, p. 1.

[7] Gammage, *op. cit.*, p. 153.

chose rather to preach upon passive obedience, and the folly of looking to the things of this life; a doctrine which only served to exasperate their hearers, who could not always be restrained from expressing their indignant feelings at the hypocrisy of the men who could preach this doctrine, while they were themselves in the enjoyment of every luxury.[1]

On one occasion

one clergyman so far forgot discretion and good feeling as to display his wit in taking for his text, " My house shall be called the house of prayer, but ye have made it a den of thieves." The Chartists quitted the church in a body upon its announcement; and thus far he triumphed; but he lost an excellent opportunity of addressing to them what might have benefited their souls.[2]

An excellent example of the sermons preached is the discourse of Dr. Whittaker to the Chartists at Blackburn. The latter requested that he preach from the first two verses of James v, " Go to now, ye rich, weep and howl for your miseries that are coming upon you. Your riches are corrupted, and your garments are moth-eaten." The clergyman complied with their request, and while admitting that these words might have fitted the old Romans, asserted that to apply them to the modern rich would be " the height of injustice and the grossest falsehood" and an "act of flagrant false witness." Especially would this accusation be untrue of England, a land " governed by equal laws, where civil rights and public guarantees of liberty are secured too firmly to be shaken except by those who enjoy their benefit." [3] Then, leaving the text, he exhorted the people to " meekness

---

[1] Gammage, *op. cit.*, p. 153.

[2] *Christian Observer*, 1839, p. 574.

[3] Whittaker, *op. cit.*, p. 9.

and endurance " and to submission and obedience to the powers that be, using Romans xiii, 1-7 and I Peter ii, 13-17 to bolster up his contentions.   Then followed the usual tirade against Chartism and the customary confusion between it and infidelity, and it and socialism.

The clergy had the courage of their convictions as well as the Chartists.   Whittaker coolly told a crowd of 4,000 that there were only 100 Chartists amongst them, the rest being simply a promiscuous crowd attracted by the public method thus used to gain notoriety.[1]   Close, in his sermon, said that this mode of approach to the house of God was " particularly offensive to the Almighty." [2]   " Nothing," said he, " is more calculated to raise the country against them or to awaken the feelings of any man who has any regard for religious decency." [3]   The *Christian Observer* called it a " mockery of divine worship " and a proceeding obviously offensive to all classes of the community.[4]   It maintained that it was absurd to say that the Chartists had as much right to go to church as other people if they proceeded thither in an orderly manner.   To allow " peaceful and devout worshippers to be put to flight by a revolutionary mob " was to obscure true liberty in technical phrases.[5]

Although the Chartists listened in many cases submissively enough to the abuses heaped upon them, for which in a measure they had themselves to blame, having put themselves in a position to receive them, disturbances ensued quite often [6] and arrests became so frequent that a defense fund

---

[1] Whittaker, *op. cit.*, p. 13.

[2] *Sermon to the Chartists*, p. 18.

[3] Close, *Female Chartists*, p. 22.

[4] *Christian Observer*, 1839, p. 573.

[5] *Ibid.*, p. 573.   For anti-Chartist sermons, *vide infra*, p. 60 *et seq.*

[6] Chartists tried to break up the meetings of Rev. Norman McLeod. McLeod, *Life of Norman McLeod* (Toronto, 1876), p. 84.

was organized, and collectors were appointed in different towns to raise subscriptions for the purpose.[1]

One of the most serious disturbances of this nature occurred at Norwich in November 1841 at the dedication of a new church. The Chartists, thinking this an excellent opportunity for a turn-out, paraded the streets with a band and many banners and proceeded to the church, which they intended to fill to the exclusion of every one else. The police, however, prevented this, but left the Chartists to obstruct the passage of other people who desired entrance. When the bishop arrived he had to be literally conveyed into the churchyard in the center of a body of police. During the preaching service the Chartist band played outside on the road to the great annoyance of those within. " Once or twice, the door being opened with a noise, the whole congregation rose in alarm for some minutes during the service." While the sermon was being preached four of the Chartists were taken into custody, a rescue was attempted and during a sharp riot in which several of the police were severely injured, one regained his freedom. During the consecration exercises, Hewitt, a prominent Chartist of that region, came up at the head of a band playing " God Save the Queen " and, making a halt in front of the church, played " Old Hundredth." The mayor and superintendent of police having apprehended Hewitt, a general rush took place in which three more Chartists were handcuffed and driven to the station house, the crowd following and threatening to pull down the prison. The prisoners were heavily fined and, in default of payment, committed to prison at hard labor. Hewitt was bound over to take his trial at the sessions.[2]

---

[1] Gammage, *op. cit.*, p. 153.

[2] *Anti-Socialist Gazette*, no. 3, p. 36, Dec. 1841.

The Chartists, of course, did not confine their operations entirely to the churches. Frequently they succeeded in monopolizing public meetings by electing their own chairman and diverting the assemblies from their original purpose. In particular they proved a thorn in the side of the Anti-Corn Law Leaguers, whose meetings were time and time again broken up by the Chartists. Their procedure was either to elect a chairman and occupy the time with their own speakers or else offer an amendment to the free-trade resolution in favor of the Charter.[1]

One of the most interesting instances of this practice occurred in December 1839 at Carlisle. A meeting was called at the Coffee House by some of the leading clergy and evangelical gentlemen,

the object of which was a " better observance of the Sabbath." Previous to the hour appointed the room was crowded with Chartists, and the original proposers of the meeting were hardly able to obtain a standing place. Nevertheless they commenced business by moving that Mr. Graham of Edmund-castle be called to the chair. This was met by an amendment that Hall, one of their own body and keeper of a pothouse in Butchergate, be elected chairman, which was carried by acclamation. The gentlemen now endeavored to retreat, but their escape was prevented, by a crowd of Chartists on every side, and they were ultimately prevailed upon to remain by an assurance from the chairman that order would be preserved, and every one should have a fair and patient hearing. So, indeed, they had—the evangelicals made their speeches, and Dr. Taylor replied in a strain of irony and abuse, full of that Chartist eloquence for which he is so remarkable. Then Julian Hardy and Cardo, and other members of the convention made their speeches, and carried two resolutions, directly opposed to the

---

[1] Prentice, *History of the Anti-Corn Law League*, vol. i, p. 192; *Memoranda of the Chartist Agitation in Dundee*, p. 28; Gammage, *op. cit.,* p. 102.

purpose for which the meeting was convened. They then passed a vote of thanks to the gentlemen for their kindness in procuring the use of the room; saying that they had always before been unsuccessful in their application for it; and concluded by making a subscription for the patriot Frost, as they styled him.[1]

As a means of advertisement this method was undoubtedly a success. As a means of protest it may have accomplished something, but in the actual promotion of the cause of the People's Charter it is probable that these interruptions did more harm than good, arousing and strengthening, as they did, the prejudices of large numbers of people.   ·

[1] *The Chartist Correspondence*, p. 8.

CHAPTER II

Chartist Substitutions for the Prevailing Christianity

I. CHRISTIAN CHARTIST CHURCHES

OF all the methods used by the Chartists to identify their movement with Christianity there was none more striking than the organization of the "Christian Chartist Churches." Disgusted with both the State and Dissenting churches for the lack of sympathy evinced by them toward their cause and convinced that neither was representing the true primitive Christianity as taught by Christ, they attempted to fill the gap; and, following the example of many before and since under similar circumstances, they started churches of their own.

At least three influences were at work upon the Chartists to induce them to organize these churches. In the first place there was the desire to draw the people away from the influence of the old churches, which were rightly judged to be hostile to their projects. "Were the Chartists to do this," said the *Circular* in regard to the founding of independent churches, "ecclesiastical tyranny would soon die a natural death, and clerical domination be banished from our land. One great obstacle to the onward progress of the present movement would thus be put out of the way." [1] In the second place there was the wish to repudiate and disprove by some active move on their part the "ecclesiastical

---

[1] *Chartist Circular*, vol. i, p. 129.

bellowing about Chartist infidelity." [1] Lastly there was undoubtedly a sincere longing to get back to fundamental principles and practices.[2]

These churches, or, as Stephens calls them, "politico-religious societies," [3] seem to have taken their rise in Scotland in the spring of 1840,[4] perhaps at the suggestion,[5] at any rate with the enthusiastic backing [6] of the *Chartist Circular*, the official publication of the Scotch Chartists.[7] This publication in its number for May 2, 1840, prints an extract from the first Chartist sermon preached in Scotland, the text being taken from the Sermon on the Mount: "Beware of false prophets," etc. The idea evidently appealed to the people, for its success was instantaneous. In August, 1840, the same paper announced enthusiastically [8] that " they have now planted their humble places of worship in almost every corner of the land ", while a year later Stephens with a little more conservatism testified to their increase.

What is most worthy of remark in the establishment of these new religious societies [said he], is that they have sprung up here and there from Scotland down to the South of England, in the absence of any previously arranged plan for their formation, and without the assistance of any missionary or proselyte-maker acting as the agent of some distant " parent society." They are not " branches " or " auxiliaries " worked from a center but separate fellow-

---

[1] *Chartist Circular*, vol. i, p. 197.

[2] *Ibid.*, p. 222; Solly, *James Woodford*, vol. ii, pp. 89 *et seq.*

[3] *The People's Magazine*, May, 1841, pp. 159 *et seq.*

[4] *Chart. Cir.*, vol. i, p. 129.

[5] *Ibid.*, p. 110.

[6] *Ibid.*, pp. 110, 129, 197, 222, 226, 374.

[7] *Ibid.*, Introduction.

[8] *Ibid.*, p. 197.

ships of the weighty and strong-minded people, who now begin in good earnest to ask what is the will of God in these things that belong as well to their earthly as to their heavenly weal.[1]

Following the successful operation of many of these churches in Scotland the idea was taken up in England where it was probably introduced by Arthur O'Neill,[2] a member of the first Central Committee of Scotland,[3] who established in Birmingham the most famous of the Christian Chartist Churches,[4] and also preached in many others.[5]

The services were held in private houses, schools, public halls,—any place where a group of people could gather. In West Bromwich, England, one of the iron masters himself lent O'Neill a large room.[6] In these places lay preachers, chosen from amongst the local societies, or Chartist "missionaries," absolutely without pay, held forth on politico-religious subjects[7] and administered the rites of baptism and the Lord's Supper and, in Scotland, marriage.[8] The usual method of procedure was to pick out some appropriate text from the Bible after the manner of a sermon, and with that as a starting point launch into a discussion of political and economic problems attempting to find the solution in the teachings of Christianity.[9] According

[1] *The People's Magazine*, p. 159.

[2] Solly, *James Woodford*, vol. ii, p. 89.

[3] *Chart. Cir.*, preface.

[4] Gammage, *op. cit.*, p. 196; Solly, *op. cit.*, pp. 89 *et seq.*; Solly, *These Eighty Years*, vol. ii, p. 222.

[5] *Parliamentary Reports*, 1843, vol. xiii, *Report of the Midland Mining Commission*, paragraphs 608 *et seq.*

[6] *Report of the Midland Mining Commission*, par. 608.

[7] *The People's Magazine*, pp. 159, 160.

[8] *Chart. Cir.*, pp. 110, 222, 226, 374.

[9] *Midland Mining Commission*, par. 610.

to the testimony of Mr. Slater, a Wesleyan minister who calls the mild-mannered and earnest O'Neill " the wretch ",[1] the latter introduced into his sermon " unmeasured abuse of Her Majesty and the Constitution, about the public expenditure, and complete radical doctrines of all kinds." [2] The Chartists had their own hymnbooks which they used at these services.[2]

The congregations were, of course, made up almost entirely of workingmen,[3] who were, in Birmingham, largely Baptist and Methodist.[4] The English operatives and colliers, when they were anything, were mostly members of these two denominations and it was principally from them that the membership of the Chartist Churches was recruited This may explain to some extent the hostility of the Methodists.

Both Churchmen and Dissenters combined to condemn these attempts to return to primitive Christianity,[5] or, to put it in their language, an attempt to set up " pretended churches, and proceeding to dispense pretended sacraments, on the ground of a political creed." [6] The opposition was due partially to loss of membership, but, especially in the case of the State Church, also to a conflict in theory of organization and polity, a church depending entirely upon lay preachers being hardly likely to commend itself to a

---

[1] *Midland Mining Commission*, par. 479.

[2] *Ibid.*, par. 608.

[3] *The People's Magazine*, May, 1841, p. 159.

[4] Solly, *James Woodford*, vol. ii, p. 90.

[5] *Mid. Min. Com.*, par. 608 *et seq.; English Review*, vol. i, p. 70; *Christian Remembrancer*, vol. v, p. 737; *British Critic*, vol. xxvii, pp. 340, 341.

[6] Marshall, *The Duty of Attempting to Reconcile the Unenfranchised with the Enfranchised Class*, p. 12.

priesthood claiming an uninterrupted succession from the Apostles.[1]

Yet these same critics admitted the success of the Chartist Churches, although seeking to explain it by the religious rather than the political element in their activities.[2] Mr. Slater testified that at West Bromwich the Chartists had a large room " which used to be crowded to suffocation every Sabbath afternoon from half-past two to a quarter past four." [3]   In Birmingham by the assiduous pursuit of all Christian duties the Chartist Church was able to live down so far the obloquy of its origin even among the wealthy classes as actually to obtain contributions from them for its work.[4]

II. EDUCATION

If the Chartists were dissatisfied with the social program of the churches in England their criticism was not of a merely negative character.   To take the place of what they considered the neglect of the church they formulated a more or less distinct plan for intellectual and social betterment. In this program the education of the masses occupied the foremost place.   According to Lovett the aim of Chartism was " to purify the heart and rectify the conduct of all, by knowledge, morality, and love of freedom." [5]   While the churches in England were squabbling as to who should control education, the Chartists stood out unequivocally for secular education.[6]   The Chartists instinctively felt that the

---

[1] *Chart. Cir.*, vol. i, pp. 374, 222.

[2] *English Review*, vol. i, p. 70; *Mid. Min. Com.*, par. 608 *et seq.*

[3] *Mid. Min. Com.*, par. 608.

[4] Solly, *James Woodford*, vol. ii, p. 90; Solly, *These Eighty Years*, vol. i, p. 383.

[5] Lovett and Collins, *Chartism*, Introduction, p. 9.

[6] *Weekly Adviser*, vol. i, p. 2; *Chartist Circular*, vol. i, p. 72; Lovett, *Life and Struggles*, pp. 141, 145, 326.

churches were more interested in the brand of religion that
was to be imparted to the children of the working classes
than either the quality of the instruction or the truthful-
ness of the knowledge.[1] Even such a representative paper
as *The Chartist Circular*, which is pervaded with a decidedly
Christian tone, bitterly denounces the education in vogue.

There is no tyranny so paralyzing to the public mind [it says],
as the despotism of priestcraft. Wherever an established
priesthood has existed, the people have been mentally and politically enslaved; and, if philosophy at any time has triumphed
over superstition it was after long and bitter struggle with
bigotry, intolerance, and selfishness of ignorant priests. If you
read the history of priestcraft in the dark ages, you will respond to my opinions. Priests have never encouraged the
people to study the truths of natural philosophy, or political
science; nor have they taught them to understand and demand
their civil, religious and natural rights.[2]

The English working class became first thoroughly
aroused on the subject of education about 1830 when the
agitation for an " Unstamped Press " became loud and persistent.[3] In this fight to remove the " tax on knowledge,"
as it was called, Henry Hetherington and John Cleave took
the leading part,[4] while their efforts were ably seconded
by such men as James Watson, William Lovett, and Bronterre O'Brien. The connection of the unstamped press
fight with the Chartist movement is easy to trace. It was
Hetherington, Cleave, Watson and Lovett who were later
the heart and soul first of " The National Union of the

[1] Lovett, *op. cit.*, p. 135.
[2] *Chartist Circular*, vol. i, p. 72; also pp. 39, 40, 59; Kingsley, *Alton Locke*, p. 47.
[3] Lovett, *Life and Struggles*, pp. 54 *et seq.*
[4] *Ibid.*, pp. 54, 91.

Working Classes and Others ",[1] then of "The London Working Men's Association," which fathered the Charter. It is interesting to note that of the six men appointed to represent the Working Men's Association in drawing up the Charter, three of them—Hetherington, Watson and Cleave —had suffered imprisonment more than once in the cause of an untaxed press.[2] Of the other three, Lovett was then prominently active, Moore later defended the same proposition,[3] while Vincent was still too young to be conspicuous

Lovett was actually engaged in educational efforts as early as 1829, when he drew up a " petition for the opening of the British Museum, and other exhibitions of Art and Nature, on Sundays." [4] In 1831 the National Union of the Working Classes and Others, which stood for universal manhood suffrage, did valiant service for the unstamped press, convinced as it was that " the wide spread poverty, the drunkenness, vices, and crimes of society were clearly traced to the absence of mental and moral light." [5] The London Workingmen's Association, founded in 1836, which launched the People's Charter, had also as its objects:

To devise every possible means, and to use every exertion, to remove those cruel laws that prevent the free circulation of thought through the medium of a cheap and honest press.

To promote by all available means the education of the rising generation and the extirpation of those systems which tend to future slavery.

To form a library of reference and useful information, etc.[6]

---

[1] Lovett, *op. cit.*, pp. 68 *et seq.*

[2] *Ibid.*, p. 62.

[3] *Ibid.*, p. 89.

[4] *Ibid.*, p. 57.

[5] *Ibid.*, p. 134.

[6] *Ibid.*, p. 93.

The connection between education and Chartism prior to 1838 is thus clearly seen. But even in the heat of the Chartist agitation the educational side was not forgotten. It was continually kept in mind by the little group of London agitators and taken up with enthusiasm in many sections. The *Weekly Adviser* pledges itself to " advocate the establishment of a national system of education on purely secular grounds." [1] *The Reformer* says that " Popular education will occupy a large share of our attention ",[2] while the *Chartist Circular* strongly urges upon the Scotch Chartists the advisability of forming schools.[3] Feargus O'Connor, who could not bear to see anything prosper which he did not originate and who represented the worst element of the movement, dubbed the educational efforts of Lovett and his friends " knowledge Chartism " and through his great influence was able to do them much harm.[4]

While imprisoned in Warwick Gaol, Lovett occupied himself with writing a little work entitled *Chartism, or a New Organization of the People*, which was published under the joint names of Lovett and Collins when they were released. In the words of Lovett:

The chief object of this work was to induce the Chartists of the United Kingdom to form themselves into a National Association for the erection of halls and schools of various kinds for the purpose of education—for the establishment of libraries; the printing of tracts; and the sending out of missionaries; with the view of forming an enlightened public opinion throughout the country in favor of the Charter, and thus better

[1] *Weekly Adviser* vol. i, p. 2.
[2] *The Reformer*, p. 1.
[3] *Chartist Circular*, p. 40.
[4] Lovett, *op. cit.*, pp. 250, 251; Gammage, *op. cit.*, p. 196.

preparing the people for the exercise of the political rights we are contending for.[1]

Lovett had figured out that if each person who signed the National Petition would contribute even less than a penny a week, in one year eighty schools at £3,000 each could be erected, equipped with playground, pleasure gardens, museums, laboratories, workshops and baths, where lectures, readings, discussions, musical entertainments and dances could be held; 710 circulating libraries at £20 each started; 4 missionaries at £200 per annum employed and 20,000 tracts per week distributed.[2] Not a mere cultivation of the intellect but a " judicious development of all their qualities "[3] was the object sought. The publication of *Chartism* was shortly followed by an address " To the Political and Social Reformers of the United Kingdom," signed by eighty-one of the leading radicals of Great Britain, including Collins, Hetherington, Cleave and Mitchell of London, urging the formation of a " National Association of the United Kingdom "[4] to carry out the projects embraced in the pamphlet of Lovett and Collins. " There was in this plan," says Gammage, " all the elements of the people's regeneration, supposing it to be faithfully and honestly carried out."[5]

Although there was no intention on the part of the promoters to oppose associations already formed,[6] the project met the bitterest opposition from O'Connor[7] and made but little headway in the provinces. It led in London, however, to the formation of a body known as " The London Members of the National Association," the first two

[1] Lovett, *op. cit.*, p. 236.
[2] *Ibid.*, p. 249, 250.
[3] *Ibid.*, p. 143.
[4] *Ibid.*, pp. 232, 236, 249.
[5] Gammage, *op. cit.*, p. 196.
[6] Lovett, *op. cit.*, p. 248.
[7] *Ibid.*, pp. 251, 255.

secretaries of which were Henry Hetherington and Charles Westerton. A weekly periodical, *The National Association Gazette*, was issued by the society [1] while in 1842 a building was rented, in which a library was installed, courses of lectures were delivered, music and dancing classes organized and in 1843 a Sunday School started.[2] A day school was finally established in 1848 through the generosity of a friend.[3]

The Chartists put themselves officially on record in 1851 when in the convention of that year they carried a proposition which " laid down the principle of national, secular, gratuitous, compulsory education." [4]

Important as was the work of the London radicals in the field of education, it was not to be compared in extent to the salutary effect on the intellectual life of the English proletariat of the great number of cheap Chartist periodicals which sprang up all over England during these years, the literary standard of which, everything considered, was remarkably high. It should also be noticed here that Joseph Barker was the editor and publisher of Barker's Library of three hundred volumes on religious, political and ethical subjects, which were up to that time the cheapest collection ever published. Indeed he is credited with being the originator of cheap literature in England.[5] Nor is the work on the lecture platform of W. J. Fox, Thomas Cooper, William Lovett, Henry Vincent, Robert Lowery and many others, covering a long period of years, to be forgotten. The purely educational effect of this alone was considerable.

[1] Lovett, *op. cit.*, p. 259.

[2] *Ibid.*, pp. 287, 288.

[3] *Ibid.*, p. 334.

[4] Gammage, *op. cit.*, p. 371.

[5] *Dictionary of National Biography*, vol. iii, pp. 205 *et seq.* This may be true of nineteenth-century literature, but Wesley was a pioneer in this field of the eighteenth. *New History of Methodism*, vol. i, p. 220.

III. TEMPERANCE AND TEETOTALISM

Chartism ought not to be considered entirely as a political movement; it contained too many elements which looked to the moral regeneration of the working classes. Next in importance to its educational phase must be reckoned its endeavor to inculcate habits of temperance and even teetotalism.

At least three motives contributed to bring the question of temperance to the front. There was in the first place an earnest desire on the part of many of the leaders of the working class to rescue their followers from the demoralizing effects on health and morals of a habit whose influence could be only too plainly seen.[1] The time and energy consumed and the money wasted in drink were a decided impediment to an efficient agitation for political rights,[2] while the ignorance and crime engendered by the excessive use of alcohol gave some ground for the accusation so often made, that the lower classes were unprepared to exercise the franchise. Last of all the Chartists believed that not only did drink help to enslave them politically by debasing them morally, but that the excise duties on liquor and tobacco actually furnished sinews of war to their oppressors.[3] The loss of revenue to the treasury which would result from abstinence on the part of the working classes from excisable articles would in the minds of many Chartists be of sufficient importance to " bring the misrule of our government to an end." [4] " We shall never get our rights," says Devildust, whom Disraeli pictures as an especially keen Chartist of the ranks, " till we leave off consuming excisable articles." [5]

---

[1] Lovett, *Life and Struggles*, pp. 57, 95; *Eng. Chart. Cir.*, pp. 6, 23, 35, etc.; *Alton Locke*, p. 84.

[2] *Eng. Chart. Cir.*, pp. 35, 46.

[3] *Ibid.*, pp. 6, 35, 40, 42, etc.

[4] *Reformer's Almanac*, p. 238.   [5] Disraeli, *Sybil*, p. 115.

Vincent, the Chartist whose name above all others is connected with the temperance agitation, sums the whole matter up when he concludes his "Address to the Working Man" with the following words:

By adopting this course, the habits of the people will be at once changed. New hopes and new desires will be awakened in the breasts of millions—intellect will start forth to dispute the arrogant pretensions of our corrupt rulers—the poorest man will derive solid benefit—myriads of wives and children will be better housed, fed, and clad—the people will become too proud to wear the degraded livery of a policeman, or to enlist as soldiers, to murder at the bidding of an aristocrat their unoffending brothers for a shilling a day—our rulers will be deprived of an immense revenue—and, to crown all, no government can long withstand the just claims of a people who have had the courage to conquer their own vices.[1]

In its connection with Chartism the agitation for temperance, like that for education, traces its beginnings to the Working Men's Association of London. As early as 1829 Lovett began to take an active interest in temperance.[2] When the London Working Men's Association was formed a few years later they sought " to make the principles of democracy as respectable in practice as they are just in theory, by excluding the drunken and immoral "[3] and those who " drown their intellect amid the drunkenness of the pot house."[4] And lest the members might succumb to temptation they avoided holding their meetings at public houses because " habit and associations are too often formed at those places which mar the domestic happiness, and de-

[1] *English Chartist Circular*, p. 35.
[2] Lovett, *Life and Struggles*, p. 57.
[3] *Ibid.*, p. 94.
[4] *Ibid.*, p. 95.

stroy the political usefulness of the millions."[1]   If no better place offered they were to meet at one another's houses.[2] Still later one reason given for the founding of the National Association of the United Kingdom[3] was the establishment of public halls where the workingmen "might be taken out of the contaminating influence of public-houses and beer-shops—places where many of their meetings are still held, in which their passions are inflamed, their reasons drowned, their families pauperized, and themselves socially degraded and politically enslaved."[4]   The same group who figured so prominently in educational efforts — Hetherington, Cleave, Lovett and Watson — in January, 1840, established *The English Chartist Circular and Temperance Advocate for England and Wales,* which was edited by James Harris and served as the official organ for the Chartist Teetotal Societies.

Vincent, who was perhaps the greatest orator which the Chartist movement produced,[5] had during his imprisonment become convinced that teetotalism was the prime requisite for success in obtaining the Charter.   Upon his release in January, 1841, he issued[6] an *Address to the Workingmen of England, Scotland, and Wales* in which he called upon them to adopt the Teetotal Pledge and " to form themselves into Chartist Teetotal Societies in every city, town and village."[7]   The address was signed by many of the most prominent Chartists in all parts of the kingdom.   Vincent followed it up by lecture tours and public propaganda of

---

[1] Lovett, *op. cit.,* p. 65.   [2] *Ibid.,* p. 96.

[3] *Ibid.,* pp. 248 *et seq.*

[4] *Ibid.,* p. 254.

[5] Gammage, *op. cit.,* p. 11.

[6] *Dictionary of National Biography,* vol. lviii, p. 359.

[7] *English Chartist Circular,* p. 35.

all kinds.   In this he was ably aided by Thomas Cooper,[1]
Rev. William Hill, Joseph Barker [2] and others, and by such
Chartist publications as the *English Chartist Circular*, the
Chartist Circular (Scotch),[3] *Reformer's Almanac*,[4] etc.
O'Connor himself was inclined to throw ridicule upon
the movement [5] but the editor of his paper, Hill, was
ardently for it [6] and O'Connor's influence was thus in a
measure neutralized.   Vincent and his followers went into
the proposition whole-heartedly.   Temperance and moder-
ate drinking they were opposed to—only absolute teetotalism would suffice.

The idea of teetotalism took hold for a time, at least, and
during the early months of 1841 numerous Chartist Teetotal Societies were formed in England which sought to
combine an advocacy of the principles of the Charter and
total abstinence.   The reports of their activities may be
partially followed in the files of the *Chartist Circular*.   At
the outset much enthusiasm was manifested and Vincent
reported the administering of the pledge to numerous followers, while Cooper in Leicester succeeded in persuading
several hundreds to " promise to abstain, etc., until the
People's Charter becomes the law of the land." [7]   Towards
the latter part of 1841 the reports cease to come in and it is
probable that the Chartist Teetotal Societies declined rapidly.
The work of the Chartist Teetotalers did, however, contribute something positive to the cause of temperance and
the general moral uplift of the English workingman.

[1] Cooper, *Life of Cooper*, pp. 164 *et seq.*
[2] *New History of Methodism*, vol. i, p. 525; *The People*, p. 1.
[3] *Chartist Circular*, pp. 285, 286.
[4] *Reformer's Almanac*, p. 238.
[5] Gammage, *op. cit.*, p. 196.
[6] *English Chartist Circular*, p. 46.
[7] Cooper, *Life of Cooper*, p. 165.

IV. OTHER REFORMS

The effort " to generate a moral stamina in the ranks of the millions " [1] was not confined to temperance and education. Alongside of these there developed a higher conception of the mission of women.[2] In an address issued by the Working Men's Association to their "working class brethren in America " Lovett writes,

We seek to make the mothers of our children fit instructors for promoting our social and political advancement, by reading and conversing with them upon all subjects we may be acquainted with; and thus by kindness and affection to make them our companions in knowledge and happiness, and not, as at present, mere domestic drudges and ignorant slaves of our passions.[3]

Their co-operation in the struggle for the Charter was welcomed and Female Chartist Societies were formed [4] which contributed not a little to the strength of the movement.[5]

Although chiefly concerned with economic and political reforms the Chartists were nevertheless usually to be found in the forefront of all progressive agitation. Thus the movement for the abolition of the death penalty found warm supporters in the Chartist ranks.[6] Militarism was particularly obnoxious, especially to those who had enjoyed a taste of it. Standing armies were declared by the London Convention of 1851 to be " contrary to the

---

[1] Lovett, op. cit., p. 133.

[2] See Lovett's " Woman's Mission "; Gammage, op. cit., p. 11.

[3] Solly, James Woodford, vol. i, pp. 75, 76.

[4] English Chartist Circular, vol. i, p. 6.

[5] Gammage, op. cit., pp. 82, 188.

[6] Dierlamm, Die Flugschriftenliteratur der Chartistenbewegung, p. 45; Gammage, op. cit., p. 372; The Reformer, p. 1.

principles of Democracy, and dangerous to the liberty of the people." [1] The group of Chartist leaders who were the backbone of the London Working Men's Association were ardent pacifists. To Lovett, speaking on behalf of the association, war was but a " barbarous means for brutalizing the people " and an instrument " to gratify aristocratic cupidity, selfishness, and ambition," [2] the result of which is to lead thousands to slaughter and to death, to increase the national debt and leave the stigma of cruelty and injustice upon the national character. " If war is the only path to civilization," cried Lovett, " what a mockery is it to preach up the religion of Christ." [3] Most of the arguments of the present-day pacifists were known and used by the Chartists.

The majority of the reforms and innovations advocated by the Chartists were obviously laudable. Others were honestly debatable. None were actually revolutionary. Their program, taken broadly, was a scheme for the political, intellectual and moral regeneration of the masses, and so it was considered by most of the reformers of the day who, perhaps, might differ as to some of the details. The attitude toward the advocates of these innovations on the part of the upper and middle classes, while not exceptional in the history of radical movements, is an interesting instance of the mind of the conservative. The prevailing feeling toward the Chartists, says Solly, was one of " horror and disgust." [4] " By highly respectable and most pious folk," observes Linton, " Chartism was considered vulgar and disreputable." [5] Although the idea of the aver-

---

[1] Gammage, *op. cit.*, pp. 371, 372.

[2] Lovett, *Life and Struggles*, pp. 265, 266.

[3] Lovett, *op. cit.*, p. 307, in *An Apology of Peace from the London Working Men's Association;* also p. 320.

[4] Solly, *These Eighty Years*, vol. i, p. 345.

[5] Linton, *Memories*, pp. 75, 76.

age Englishman in regard to Chartism was undoubtedly very hazy,[1] he was sure it was something evil and to be avoided. To become associated with " the lawless demo- crats " and " the enemies of law and order," as they were frequently called, entailed usually the loss of the friend- ship of former associates and frequently of the means of livelihood itself.[2] To advocate political freedom at a time when Europe was restless with revolution, secular education at a time when instruction was largely exploited by sectarian interests, teetotalism when intoxicating liquors were the or- dinary beverage of all, and the separation of church and state at just the time when the influence of the Oxford movement was beginning to make itself felt, was to arouse the bitter antagonism of all classes. The aristocracy and bourgeoisie found the whole subject too painful to contem- plate and sought refuge in government prosecutions and in the abridgement of common-law liberties. Yet the Chart- ists, who had found in this agitation for political, economic, social and religious reformation a substitute for religious enthusiasm, firmly believed that they were not only trying to fulfill the teachings of Christ but were actually engaged in a work which rightfully belonged to the church.

[1] Parker, *A Preacher's Life*, p. 16.

[2] *Contemporary Review*, May, 1904, p. 733; Solly, *These Eighty Years*, vol. i, pp. 394, 398.

CHAPTER III

Attitude of the Churches Toward Chartism

I. THE CHURCH OF ENGLAND

A. The Church as a Whole

THE unsavory reputation which the clergymen of the Established Church had acquired amongst the political radicals [1] was, on the whole, deserved. With even more vehemence than they had manifested against the Reform Bill of 1832 they now took up the fight against Chartism. Almost as one man they stood opposed to further extension of the suffrage and the Chartists recognized in the clergymen of the Church of England their bitterest enemies.

This clerical opposition was first naturally expressed in the most convenient means at hand. Innumerable sermons were preached on such subjects as " The Sin of Despising Dominion," [2] " Great Britain's Happiness," [3] " The Powers that be are Ordained of God," [4] " Obedience to Lawful Authority," [5] " Fear God and Honor the King," [6] etc. Of the printed political sermons some mention Chartism by name

---

[1] *Supra*, pp. 20 *et seq.*

[2] Sermon of Rev. John Haigh, M. A., reviewed in *The People*, p. 39.

[3] Sermon of Rev. Robert Sutton, Canon Redemptionary of Ripon, reviewed in *The People*, p. 169.

[4] Sermon of Rev. J. Slade, of Bolton, reviewed in *The People*, p. 283.

[5] Sermon of Rev. E. B. Were, *Ch. of Eng. Mag.*, vol. x, p. 216.

[6] Disraeli, *Sybil*, p. 392.

and some only by implication but all are " published with
the view of checking the spread of democratic principles
and the growth of democratic feeling." ¹   They seldom attempt to argue out the proposition but are characterized by
the most indiscriminate denunciation of all political reformers, who are referred to as " children of the devil; as bad,
immoral, and unprincipled men; as filthy dreamers," and the
like.²

A number of sermons were preached expressly on Chartism, usually upon the visit to a church of the Chartists
in a body.³   Some half-dozen of these sermons were printed
and had a large circulation, being distributed as tracts by
the Religious Tract Society.⁴   One of them has already
been briefly examined.⁵   It will suffice to glance at another,
that by the Rev. Evan Jenkins, Incumbent Minister of Dowlais, entitled *Chartism Unmasked,* which, according to
the title page, reached nineteen editions.   Jenkins begins
by affirming that " The doctrines taught and urged by the
Chartist leaders, are as diametrically opposed to the doctrines revealed in the eternal word of God, as the North is
to the South." ⁶   " The Chartist leaders," says he, " preach
and teach the doctrine of ' equality '; but we have no such
doctrine taught us by the Book of Nature or the Book of
God."   After illustrating inequality in nature he shows
how it exists in every field of human life and government,
quoting Exodus XVIII. 20, 21, 22; Judges II. 16; I Samuel II. 7; Proverbs VIII. 15; 16; Daniel III.; and Romans
XIII. 1, to prove that the doctrine of " gradations " has

¹ *The People,* p. 169.
² *Ibid.,* p. 39.
³ *Supra,* pp. 35 *et seq.*
⁴ *Chartist Circular,* p. 193.
⁵ *Supra,* p. 37.
⁶ Jenkins, *Chartism Unmasked,* pp. 5 *et seq.*

ATTITUDE OF THE CHURCHES61

the divine sanction. The second Chartist doctrine opposed to the word of God, he continues, is " the following, namely, that poverty is not the result of the everlasting purpose of a Sovereign God, but is only the result of unjust human laws, and of the oppression of unfeeling, selfish, hard-hearted, and grinding rich men." This is disproved also by the Bible which says that " The poor shall never cease out of the land." "Ask yourself who is right and who is wrong?", cries Jenkins, " the all-wise God or the Chartist leaders."

The points of the Charter were, in his mind, easily disposed of. Annual parliaments meant simply " annual squabbles, annual turmoils, annual upsetting and destruction of the peace, tranquillity, unity and trade of the country." [1] Universal suffrage would bring nothing but universal confusion with father divided against son and the mother against the daughter. " Vote by ballot would be nothing but a law for rogues and knaves, nothing but a cloak for dishonesty, insincerity, hypocrisy and lies!" To pay members of Parliament would only make inefficient members more idle and would turn the Parliament into a group of adventurers whose whole interest would be, "How to advance their own wages."

Not only is poverty appointed by God, said Jenkins, but so also is " work and labour " (Genesis III. 19; Exodus xx. 9). But if God has ordained poverty and labor he has also made abundant provision for the present comfort and eternal happiness of the poor: (1) He has commanded the rich to contribute liberally toward their wants (Deut. xv. 7-11; VI. 17-19; I John III. 17-18); (2) God himself has promised that the pious poor shall have a sufficiency (Psalm LXVIII. 10; CXXXII. 10; Isaiah XLI. 17; Matt. VI. 26,

[1] Jenkins, *Chartism Unmasked*, pp. 10 *et seq.*

28-30); (3) God has made a further and better provision for the poor, a spiritual one, because (a) Jesus was poor; (b) the ministry of Christ was in a peculiar manner the ministry of the poor (Matth. xi. 4-6); (c) the salvation of the poor is much easier to obtain than that of the rich (Mark x. 23; Romans ii. 4-6; 1 Tim. vi. 9; 1 Cor. i. 26-28; James ii. 5).

Having established this relationship between the Gospel and the poor he entreated the people that they turn from the Chartist leaders,[1] cease from reading " their inflammatory publications—publications that speak as highly of Tom Paine as they do of Jesus Christ!", that they " never attend Chartist and political meetings ", and " have nothing to do with secret societies and secret oaths ", that they " never, except upon some urgent business, be seen in one of the beer houses ", and above all that they should " embrace religion." He closes with a plea for an adequate number of churches and devoted ministers. The Church of England, he says, " and Chartism totally oppose each other ",[2] and

a sufficient number of churches, with the blessing of God accompanying and resting upon the ministrations of His servants, would soon prove an invincible barrier to the progress of Chartism, and all similar proceedings; and, would cause them to wither and die, by changing the minds, the feelings, the hearts, and consequently the actions of the people.

These sermons, of course, did not go unchallenged. The *Chartist Circular* printed a series of three articles, each entitled "A Tilt with the Parsons ",[3] while Joseph Barker in

[1] Jenkins, *Chartism Unmasked*, pp. 22 et seq.
[2] Appendix III.
[3] *Chartist Circular*, pp. 193, 205, 237.

a series of five articles in *The People* [1] reviews a sermon by
Rev. John Haigh, of Huddersfield, and in eight articles [2]
headed "Our Admirable Constitution in Church and
State," takes the Rev. Robert Sutton, Canon Redemptionary
of Ripon, to task for his sermon on "Great Britain's Happiness." With such a skilled political controversialist
as Barker the clergy could hardly hope to hold their own.
Although the Chartists did not have Romans XIII. to serve
as a basis for their arguments, they had what was of much
more practical value, namely, a fairly accurate idea of the
actual state of the country politically and economically. In
the mere matter of abuse and the calling of names the Chartists proved as facile as the clergy.

In addition to sermons, several pamphlets appeared from
the pens of Anglican clergymen. The Rev. Hugh Stowell,
M. A., in his pamphlet, *No Revolution: A Word to the
People of England*, with the Biblical text, "Meddle not
with them that are given to change", on the title page,[3]
strikes a new chord when he appeals against the Chartists on
the ground that many of their leaders are Irish Papists—
Jesuits perhaps. Others are traders in agitation. He maintains that there is no slavery in England, nor is there one
law for the rich and another for the poor. If some of the
workingmen are starving it is no fault of the masters, for
the interests of both are identical. He closes in the customary strain: "May you never cast off your reverence
for that Book which teaches you that 'the powers that be
are ordained of God', and that 'he that resisteth the power,
resisteth the ordinance of God'! May you never set at
naught the counsel of the wisest of men, 'Fear God and

[1] *The People*, pp. 39, 45, 73, 105, 113.

[2] *Ibid.*, pp. 169, 177, 185, 201, 219, 233, 246, 289; see also p. 283.

[3] Third edition, Manchester, 1848.

the King; and meddle not with them that are given to change '." [1]

Another anti-Chartist pamphlet is entitled, *A Few Words to the Chartists by a Friend.* Says the author, as he begins, I must

at once tell you the worst of myself—those particulars, I mean, which may incline you the most to dislike and suspect

[1] This was immediately answered in a pamphlet entitled, *Is There One Law for the Rich and Another for the Poor? Being a Reply by a Working Man to 'No Revolution' lately published by the Rev. Hugh Stowell.* On the title-page appears the text, "When the righteous are in authority the people rejoice; but when the wicked beareth rule the people mourn."—Prov. xxix, 2. The Working Man answers that it is unfair to raise the cry of "No Popery" to stifle public opinion. He calls it slavery for a large class "to produce and yet have not," and "for the working bees to toil, and procure honey for the idle drones to devour." That there is class legislation, he says, is only too evident, and the most deplorable feature of the whole affair is that the clergymen of the Established Church are responsible for it. In answer to the plea for "patience" and "trust in God," he answers: "Patience ought to have its limits, and that in addition to trust in God he ought to have his powder dry. The Bible tells us having food and raiment, therewith be content, but does not say having neither food or raiment we must be content" (p. 6). Then follows a refutation of the biblical quotations used by Stowell with a number of texts to strengthen the other side. In summing up he says: '"That good subjects ought to have good government, that the laws of England ought to be in accordance with the laws of God, that the working man is stamped as much in the image of his Creator as the terrible and proud aristocrat, repeat that beautiful passage from Holy Writ contained in the second chapter of Malachi. It reads thus: 'Have we not all one father? hath not one God created us?—then why do we deal treacherously, every one with his brother, by profaning the covenant of our fathers?' Do not tell us that divine providence has placed us in this wretched situation, while we know that it is base and wicked laws, made by base and wicked men. Do not show us the rough and thorny way to heaven, while you yourself the primrose path of dalliance tread. If our reward in heaven is to be in proportion to our sufferings on earth, if the greater our tribulations here, the greater our reward hereafter, tell the rich churchmen and over-paid parsons to change situations with us, and great will be *their* reward in heaven" (pp. 7, 8).

me. I am an old man: and therefore, you may probably con-
clude, fixed in all notions, and desirous to keep all matters as
they are—I also am a clergyman; and consequently you may
set me down as a bigoted partisan in all church concerns.—
Again: I am an elector; and so may be disposed to have no
disposition to increase the number—and, farther, I am in the
middle class of society.[1]

He is opposed to all points of the Charter. The people,
he says, do not know enough to vote and would not send
the best men to represent them. As to property qualification, those having property are the best to make laws concerning it. What is the use of paying members when you
can get good men to serve for nothing? Annual parliaments would unnecessarily stir up the country. Secret
ballot would not prove secret and it would separate the
member from his constituents. He would hold the suffrage
from the uneducated but he " distinctly and solemnly " [2]
states that he imputes no blame to the working class because of their ignorance.

Still another was a tract by the Vicar of Rotherham
entitled *Modern Politicians: A Word to the Working
Classes of Great Britain*. The object of this pamphlet, according to Barker, appeared to be "to support existing evils,
by throwing reproach and ridicule on the advocates of reform ".[3]

The prevailing feeling among the clergy of the State
Church was echoed in its papers representing both the High
and Low Church schools. On examining the High Church
papers it is discovered that the *Christian Guardian and
the Church of England Magazine* is concerned because
Satan and the " emissaries of evil " are spreading " political discontent and impatience of the control of religion "

[1] P. 3.   [2] P. 11.
[3] *Reformer's Almanac*, p. 353.

in the manufacturing districts.[1] To the *Christian Remembrancer,* " Radicalism and Chartism are impossible for Christians and Churchmen ", and, they trust, for England.[2] The *English Review* admits that,

It is a sad but certain truth that vast masses of our labouring population, some hundreds of thousands in number, are banded together in an association, which professes, for the moment, only to seek for Universal Suffrage, and the centralization of all power in the working classes; but which at the same time demonstrates, through all its organs, its impatient eagerness to overthrow every institution of our country and create an absolute despotic democracy on the ruins of individual freedom and imperial greatness.[3]

Liberty, according to the *English Review,* is synonymous with division of power, and it is under this liberty that the people now live. If the middle classes have the House of Commons and the aristocracy the House of Lords, the unfranchised have great power too, " being directly represented by public meetings, the right of petition, the show of hands at nomination, the press, *etc.*" It is therefore the duty of all to teach the laboring classes to prefer " the true individual freedom which they at present enjoy " to a political change which would bring only " democratic despotism." [4] Three years later, in 1851, this same paper feels called upon to dispel the " agreeable delusion " that Chartism is defunct. It is more dangerous than ever now, it asserts, because orderly. " For we have nothing to fear from democracy, the pike in its hand, everything from its gradual, and, if we may say ' constitutional ' demolition of our Constitution in Church and

---

[1] Vol. for 1847, p. 332.   [2] Vol. viii, p. 683.

[3] Vol. ix, pp. 194, 195.

[4] *English Review,* vol. ix, pp. 194-196.

State." [1] Any increase of the suffrage is to be dreaded as tending to establish the supreme authority in a single branch of the legislature, thus upsetting the equilibrium of balance of power. [2]

The Low Church organs were equally hostile. Although the *Church of England Magazine* attributed the riots of 1842 to a lack of religion which would have made the operatives " satisfied with their position in life," [3] it still had a wholesome fear of Chartism. [4] The editor of the *Christian Observer* was greatly alarmed over the " Chartists and the very refuse of society who cannot, or will not, distinguish between the excellency of an institution and the casual temporary defects of its administration ", [5] and in the year 1839 he mentions them almost every month in the department called " View of Public Affairs ". [6] The secular reviews like the *Quarterly* and the *Edinburgh,* which contained, however, numerous religious articles, were in a similar manner opposed to Chartism. [7]

Sometimes in the daily rounds of pastoral duty a clergyman would find an opportunity to express his feelings in regard to the Chartist demands. Rev. J. T. Brown of Northampton, upon finding a Chartist tract in the house of a parishioner, tore out six leaves and threw them in the fire, afterwards asserting that any other tracts found in his district teaching sedition and blasphemy would be treated in a similar manner. [8] Joseph Parker tells of one man who

[1] *English Review,* vol. xvi, p. 56.

[2] *Ibid.,* vol. xvi, p. 85. See also *British Critic,* vol. xxvii, pp. 340, 341.

[3] *Church of England Magazine,* vol. xvi, p. 368.

[4] *Ibid.,* vol. xx, p. 215.   [5] *Christian Observer,* vol. lix, p. 446.

[6] *Ibid.,* pp. 381, 446, 510, 640, 817, and especially 573.

[7] *Quarterly Review,* vol. lxv, pp. 483 *et seq.;* vol. lxvi, pp. 461 *et seq.;* vol. lxxxv, p. 293; vol. lxxxix, pp. 491 *et seq.*

[8] *The People,* vol. i, p. 333.

proposed that the *Northern Star* be taken into a public news room, upon which " he was expelled for his insolence, the vicar and several persons of property passing him on the road as if he had lost any little character which he might have had." [1]

Kingsley, when he drew what he considered a type of the average Church of England clergyman of high rank, put in his mouth the words, " What's that about brotherhood and freedom, Lillian? We don't want anything of that kind here." [2] It was exactly that attitude which separated so decidedly the clergy from the working-class radicals. It is true that in the opposition to the New Poor Law and in the fight against the factory system an occasional point of contact was established. In the struggle for a greater democracy in church and state and in the emphasis placed upon Christianity the Chartists found little in common with the Church of England or its representatives.

B. The High Church or Oxford Movement

Although the chief influence of the High Church movement was felt along theological and doctrinal lines, yet there was in it a distinctly political element which it is impossible to ignore.[3] This political feature was particularly in evidence during the early years of that movement, for the political situation then called it into being. The Reform Bill of 1832 developed two distinct parties in the English Church, one of which decided to accept the inevitable and make the best of it, the other, later developing into the High Church Party, was " opposed to liberalism in church and state ",[4] and was unwilling to remain passive under the attacks of the government.

[1] Parker, *A Preacher's Life*, p. 54.   [2] *Alton Locke*, p. 154.

[3] Tulloch, *Movement of Religious Thought in Britain during the Nineteenth Century*, p. 105.

[4] *Ibid.*, p. 88.

To this party the Reform Bill had come as a horrible night-mare, and was looked upon as a logical sequence to the anti-church measures already passed.[1] The composition of the first reformed parliament was not such as to allay their fears, and the ministry itself was thought to be " connected with all that was dangerous in religious principle, zealous friends of Rationalists, Deists, Socinians, Dissenters, and Roman Catholics, all of whom were equally bent on the destruction of the Church."[2] The fears of Churchmen that further measures detrimental to the Establishment might be introduced were soon confirmed. Early in 1833[3] the government in consequence of a motion of Mr. Ward, member for St. Albans, brought in a bill to reduce the number of Irish bishops from twenty-two to twelve, and to tax the Irish clergy and apply the proceeds to the extinction of *church-cess*, a rate levied to keep the church buildings in good condition. It was this bill with the accompanying admonition of Lord Grey to the prelates to set their house in order that galvanized the High Church Party into action and caused the founding in 1833 of the " Association of Friends of the Church ",[4] the beginning of the Oxford Movement and the publication of the *Tracts for the Times*. These circumstances led Dean Stanley to ascribe to the movement an " origin entirely political ".[5] The followers of Pusey and R. H. Froude fought every hostile movement on the part of the government, to the extent of

[1] The High Churchmen looked upon the repeal of the Test and Corporation Acts of 1828 and the Catholic Emancipation Act of 1829 as anti-church measures. *Vide* Overton, *The Anglican Revival*, p. 9.

[2] Palmer, *Narrative of Events Connected with the Publication of Tracts for the Times*, p. 38.

[3] *Ibid.*, pp. 44, 101; Molesworth, *History of England*, vol. i, p. 286.

[4] Palmer, *op. cit.*, pp. 95 *et seq.*

[5] Church, *The Oxford Movement*, pp. 1, 2, note; *Edinburgh Review*, 1880, pp. 309, 310.

opposing in 1836 the reform of the English Church,[1] and
so exerted an influence political as well as spiritual.[2]

The politics of the Oxford Movement were ultra-Tory.
Froude " was a Tory of the old Cavalier stamp." [3]   To
Newman, revolutionary Paris was so distasteful that he
kept indoors when his boat stopped at Algiers so as not to
look upon the Tricolor.[4]   Keble was a " Tory of the Old
School ".[5]   Ward in his college days at Oxford moved at
the Union: " That an absolute monarchy is a more desir-
able form of government than the constitution proposed by
the Reform Bill of Lord John Russell ".[6]   Rose, Palmer
and Percival were equally conservative.[7]   In fact to be a
High Churchman was synonymous with being a Tory.[8]

" It was a new Toryism or designed to be such, as well as a
new sacerdotalism ",[9] says Professor Tulloch.   It was indeed a new Toryism of a particularly vital kind, not a
mere helpless attempt to maintain the *status quo*.   The
glories of the medieval state as pictured by Scott [10] and of
the medieval church as drawn by Ward in *The Ideal Church*
seem to have been continually before the minds of the
Oxford leaders.   With " its bases in a deep distrust of
democracy ", " the High Church party stood for the asser-

[1] Palmer, *op. cit.*, p. 63.

[2] *Ibid.*, pp. 105 *et seq.*

[3] Newman, *Apologia*, p. 48 (Everyman's Library edition).

[4] Tulloch, *op. cit.*, p. 105.

[5] *Ibid.*, p. 87; also *Letters and Correspondence*, ed. by Anne Mozley,
p. 32.

[6] Ward, *William Ward and the Oxford Movement*, p. 20.

[7] Overton, *The Anglican Revival*, p. 32.

[8] Mozley, *Reminiscences Chiefly of Oriel College and the Oxford
Movement*, vol i, p. 188.

[9] Tulloch, *op. cit.*, p. 105.

[10] *British Critic*, April, 1839, vol. xxv, p. 399.

tion of paternalism in government " and " of a more or less
paternal ecclesiasticism ".[1] The Catholic idea that unques-
tioning obedience is a virtue in itself was firmly embedded
in the doctrine of Puseyism. A reverence for authority,
especially ecclesiastical, was fundamental, while unstinted
condemnation was meted out to the spirit of lawlessness of
the times.[2] The attitude of the Oxford Movement to the
liberalism of the day is nowhere better set forth than in
the first part of Tract 83, published in 1840, where most of
the reform projects of the time are ascribed to Satan's
efforts to bring about an apostasy from the Church of
Christ. It says:

He promises you civil liberty; he promises you equality; he
promises you trade and wealth; he promises you a remission
of taxes; he promises you reform. This is the way he con-
ceals from you the kind of work to which he is putting you;
he tempts you to rail against your rulers and superiors; he
does so himself, and induces you to imitate him; or he promises
you illumination—he offers you knowledge, science, philosophy,
enlargement of mind. He scoffs at times gone by, he scoffs
at every institution that reveres them," etc.[3]

These are the characteristics of the " Times of Antichrist "
to which the Oxford Movement is unalterably opposed.

But not only did Puseyism have political antecedents and
teach a definite political doctrine but it had its recognized
ally in the political arena of the day. Partially through its
influence a new party was growing up, known as " Young
England ". What the Oxford Movement would do for the

---

[1] Hall, *Social Meaning of Modern Religious Movements in England*,
pp. 219, 222, 230.

[2] *Ibid.*, p. 229; *Tracts for the Times*, no. 86, pp. 39, 50, 84 *et seq.*, and
no. 87, p. 121.

[3] *Tracts for the Times*, no. 83, pp. 13, 14.

Church, Young England would do for the state.[1] Repudiating Conservatism, Whiggism and Radicalism as all alike inadequate to the needs of the time the Young England Party, like the Oxford, stood for a new Toryism, a Toryism with a program. An examination of the platform of the Young England Party as promulgated by Disraeli in his *Sybil* (1844) and *Coningsby* (1845) shows an unmistakable affinity between the purposes of the two movements, which was generally conceded at the time.[2] In secular politics Young England would abolish class legislation, recognize the authority of public opinion and restore to the sovereign his lost prerogatives,[3] attaining progress without change in the form of government.[4] In ecclesiastical matters they would restore the church to its medieval glory of freedom from the state, of emphasis upon forms, of democracy and of friendship for the people.[5]

To Young England the social question was a most important one. The attitude of this group is unmistakably expressed in Disraeli's Chartist novel, *Sybil or The Two Nations*. Stirred by what he considered the two great evils of the time, namely, " the oppression of the church and the degradation of the people ",[6] Disraeli held that the working class, as a class, were entitled to certain privileges as much as any class in England and those privileges consisted of at least food, clothing and shelter. In support of this he said:

the rights of labor were as sacred as those of property; that if a difference were to be established, the interests of the

---

[1] *Edinburgh Review*, vol. 81, pp. 504, 505.

[2] *Christian Remembrancer*, June, 1844, p. 678.

[3] Disraeli, *Sybil*, pp. 314, 489.   [4] *Ibid.*, p. 335.

[5] *Eclectic Magazine*, 1844, p. 51.

[6] Disraeli, *Sybil*, pp. 67, 69, 128, 129.

living ought to be preferred . . . the social happiness of the millions should be the first object of a statesman, and that, if this were not achieved, thrones and dominions, the pomp and power of courts and empires, were alike worthless.[1]

He would " bring back strength to the Crown, liberty to the Subject, and announce that power has only one duty; to secure the social welfare of the People ".[2] This prosperity of the people he would bring back not by increasing the franchise but by educating the wealthy and the churches up to a sense of their duty. The nobility should look upon the tenantry as human beings rather than as so much wealth, while the church, as in the middle ages, should turn to wholesale and lavish charity. The noble was to be " father of the poor and chief of the neighborhood ". Disraeli's ideas were taken up enthusiastically by many. " Doles were formally given out at stated hours to all who would come for them at the castle gate ",[3] while " Young noblemen played cricket with the peasants on their estates and the Saturnian age was believed by a good many to be returning." [4] In other words the whole scheme was that of a great paternal and benevolent despotism. Disraeli has infinite sympathy for the poor and oppressed, but no faith in Chartism as a means of bettering their lot.

Although the combination of the activities of these two parties, the State and Church Puseyites, caused an outbreak of social activity and philanthropic work similar to that accompanying the Methodist revival,[5] yet this was not what the Chartists wanted. Undoubtedly the idea of Dis-

[1] Disraeli, *Sybil*, p. 337.   [2] *Ibid.*, p. 315.
[3] McCarthy, *A History of Our Own Times*, vol. i, p. 328.
[4] *Ibid.*, vol. i, p. 329.
[5] Hall, *op. cit.*, pp. 221, 224, 225; Palmer, *op. cit.*, pp. 258, 259.

raeli's paternal despotism might have appealed to such men as Stephens or even O'Connor or O'Brien,[1] but it had no place in the thought of the school of Lovett. Dierlamm well says: " The striving toward social, political and intellectual independence of the workers—one of the fundamental principles of Chartism—stood diametrically opposed to the thought of Disraeli ".[2] The *Times* newspaper, which was considered as the special mouthpiece of the Young England party,[3] was most bitterly hated by the Chartists.[4]

There was, however, a superficial similarity between the ideas of one group of Chartists, and the followers of the Oxford Movement and Young England in at least one respect. Dierlamm makes a strong point when he maintains that the real division in the Chartist ranks was not that between the physical and moral force wings (this division is to be found in all movements), but in the division between those who, like O'Connor and O'Brien, were forever looking backward to the former prosperous days of the English laborer and seeking to restore conditions which had forever passed away, and those who, like Lovett and Cooper, accepted the changes of the industrial revolution and sought a remedy in the intellectual and moral development and regeneration of the workingman.[5] It was the futile endeavor to bring back the good old days, which probably never existed, and the continuous looking backward that bound in a measure one group of Chartists to the

[1] Dierlamm, *Die Flugschriftenliteratur der Chartistenbewegung*, p. 19.

[2] *Ibid.*, p. 87. " Das Streben nach zozialen, politischen und intellectuellen Selbstandigheit des Arbeiters—eine des Grundideen des Chartismus—stand der Gedanken Disraeli's diametral entgegen."

[3] *Ed. Rev.*, vol. lxxxi, p. 504.

[4] Dierlamm, *op. cit.*, p. 80.

[5] Dierlamm, *op. cit.*, p. 9.

two aristocratic [1] movements in church and state. But the average Chartist wanted first political justice, thinking that having once acquired this, he would be in a position to demand and obtain social justice. With the ultra-Toryism and the benevolent despotism of the Oxford Movement and Young England, Chartism had always little sympathy. One Chartist, Charles Westerton, " rendered great service to the Liberal cause by his opposition to Puseyism ",[2] while Lovett and other leaders were equally hostile. The whole Chartist conception of Christian worship as exemplified in their religious dogma [3] and in the Chartist Churches [4] was the exact opposite to that held by the Oxford Movement and its allies in parliament.

C. The Broad Church

While the High Churchmen, sighing for an idealistic medievalism, sought a solution for the social problem in a return to the conditions of bygone days, another branch of the Church of England with a viewpoint more practical was making itself felt. This was the Broad Church movement, which traces its line from Coleridge and Arnold through Maurice and Kingsley to Ruskin and Toynbee. The leaders of this school were actuated by a willingness to accept the inevitable developments in science and democracy,[5] but meant, if possible, to bring them in line with Christianity.

What transformed the Broad Church movement from the dilettante musings of a few philosophically inclined

[1] Palmer, *op. cit.*, p. 60.

[2] Lovett, *op. cit.*, p. 259.

[3] *Supra*, pp. 19 *et seq.*

[4] *Supra*, pp. 42 *et seq.*

[5] *Charles Kingsley: His Letters and Memories of His Life*, vol. i, p. 141.

literary men and ministers to a vital factor in the life of
England was the almost incredible growth of infidelity particularly amongst the working classes. The real struggle
of the day, said Maurice, was between Atheism and Christ,[1]
while Kingsley thought that in the approaching political
and social crisis, " religion, like a rootless plant, may be
brushed away in the struggle ".[2]   The workingmen, wearied with the cant phrases of the orthodox churchmen and
disgusted with their unwillingness or failure to meet
squarely the questions of the religious radicals from Paine
and Priestley to Mill and Holyoake, seemed to be drifting
entirely away from the influence of the church. " In plain
truth," said Kingsley, " the English clergy must Arnold-
ize, if they do not wish to go either to Rome or to the work-
house, before fifty years are out ".[3]   It was toward an
attempt to reconcile science and religion and to win the free-
thinkers back that the Broad Churchmen directed their
activities.

In the purely intellectual field such men as Whately,
Arnold of Rugby, Hampden, Stanley, Milman and Thirl-
wall rendered " vast assistance to men struggling with the
evident contradictions between modern criticism, history,
and philosophy and the systems of religious belief common
in their day ".[4]   But the inevitable alliance of liberalism
in politics and religion soon drew the attention of the
Broad Church leaders to the social problem, for " the now
threatening danger of English life was the identification of
all social change with extreme radicalism in religion ".[5]
This truth seems to have been first intensely felt by Fred-

[1] *Charles Kingsley*, vol. i, p. 142.   [2] *Ibid.*, vol. i, p. 142.
[3] *Ibid.*, vol. i, p. 143.
[4] Hall, *op. cit.*, p. 181.
[5] *Ibid.*, p. 182.

erick Denison Maurice, but the facts were so obvious and
the need for action so great that he was soon surrounded
by an ardent band of co-workers, the most important of
whom were Charles Kingsley, Archdeacon Hare, William
Ludlow and Thomas Hughes,[1] while Robertson of Brighton, although not in sympathy with the socialism of these
men, held closely to their views in other respects.[2]

This group had been considering for some time the best
method of approach to the workingmen, when the revolution of 1848 on the Continent and the renewed activity of
the Chartists at home gave them an opportunity which they
at once seized. To the Chartists, disappointed after the
fiasco on Kennington Common, Kingsley came with his
appeal of April 12th.[3] This was followed on May 6th by
the first number of *Politics for the People*,[4] to which
Maurice, Kingsley, Ludlow, Archdeacon Hare, Professor
Conington, Archbishop Whately and Sir Arthur Helps
were important contributors.[5] *Politics for the People*
(1848) was far from being a Chartist publication; it was
almost conservative. Physical Force Chartism was de-
nounced even to the extent of condemning monster meetings, whether lawful or not, as senseless and criminal,[6] and
" the demand for universal suffrage by men who had neither
education or moral self-government to qualify for the
vote "[7] was vigorously opposed.

[1] Seligman, "Owen and the Christian Socialists," *Political Science
Quarterly*, vol. i, pp. 221, 239.

[2] Brooke, *Life and Letters of Frederick W. Robertson*, chap. ix.

[3] Appendix VI; *Charles Kingsley*, vol. i, pp. 156, 157.

[4] *Charles Kingsley*, vol. i, p. 162; Maurice, *Life of Frederick D.
Maurice*, vol. i, p. 474.

[5] Seligman, *op. cit.*, p. 226.

[6] *Life of Maurice*, vol. i, p. 472.

[7] *Charles Kingsley*, vol. i, p. 162.

The relationship of such men as Maurice, Kingsley, and Robertson to the Chartist movement is easily misunderstood. It is true that Kingsley wrote a Chartist novel in which he pleaded passionately for justice to the lower classes, and he and Maurice addressed frequent groups of Chartists,[1] as did Robertson.[2] But not one of the three had any faith in Chartism as a political creed, or believed that the Six Points would remedy the social evils or materially ameliorate the lot of the workingman. Maurice speaks of the "unrighteous pretensions"[3] of Chartism and offers himself as a special constable for the 10th of April.[4] Robertson admits that the Chartists refused to own him as a brother.[5] It is true that Kingsley proclaimed himself a Chartist one time at a public meeting,[6] but he never advocated any of its points or apparently had any faith in them. As he himself said, "But my quarrel with the Charter is, that it does not go far enough in reform." He was not bitterly opposed to it; he simply thought that, as a method of reform, it failed to touch the real need of the people. He chides the Chartists with the mistake "of fancying that legislative reform is social reform, or that men's hearts can be changed by Act of Parliament", and goes on to say:

If anyone will tell me of a country where a charter made the rogues honest, or the idle industrious, I shall alter my opinion of the Charter, but not till then. It disappointed me bitterly when I read it. It seemed a harmless cry enough, but a poor, bald, constitutionmongering cry as I ever heard. That French

---

[1] *Charles Kingsley*, vol. i, pp. 205 *et seq.; Life of Maurice*, vol. i, pp. 519, 536, 537, 538, 539, 542.

[2] Brooke, *Life of Robertson*, Appendix, pp. 743, 748.

[3] *Life of Maurice*, vol. i, p. 278.   [4] *Ibid.*, p. 472.

[5] *Life*, p. 170.

[6] *Charles Kingsley*, vol. i, p. 166.

cry of " Organization of Labour " is worth a thousand of it, and yet that does not go to the bottom of the matter by many a mile.[1]

In *Alton Locke* the failure of Chartism does not concern him greatly. In fact he looks upon it almost as a just retribution for the sins of the Chartists, and as an event which should bring them back to better and more certain ways of gaining their rights.[2]

What then had the Broad Churchmen to offer the lower classes in place of the Charter? Two things primarily— education and coöperation. In January, 1840, Maurice said that Chartism " could only be crushed by education ".[3] Robertson's advice was: "Reform yourselves and institutions will reform themselves." [4] " Workers of England," wrote Kingsley, " be wise, and then you *must* be free, for then you will be *fit* to be free." [5] The emphasis was upon a reform of the individual not upon the government. A practical beginning in education was made at Little Ormond Yard, " a place so disorderly that no policeman liked to venture there at night ".[6] By 1860, Workingmen's Colleges were established in at least eleven cities.[7] The educational work of Toynbee Hall, of Morris and of Ruskin was in a measure an outgrowth of the efforts of Maurice and his fellow-laborers.[8]

As a more immediate method of alleviation, Maurice and

[1] *Charles Kingsley*, vol. i, p. 163.
[2] *Alton Locke*, chap. xl.
[3] *Life of Maurice*, vol. i, p. 278.
[4] Brooke, *Life of Robertson*, p. 748.
[5] *Charles Kingsley*, vol. i, p. 157.
[6] *Life of Maurice*, vol. i, p. 482.
[7] *Ibid.*, vol. i, p. 378.
[8] Hall, *op. cit.*, p. 197.

Kingsley, aided by Ludlow, Hughes and others, proposed coöperation. They called themselves "Christian Socialists" and desired to organize the trades into coöperative societies on a Christian basis. A beginning was made with the tailors in 1850,[1] and several societies were formed. Although coöperation has made progress in England these organizations soon disappeared. The history of the Christian Socialists and their activities resembles closely that of the London Working Men's Association, whose early coöperative efforts eventually gave way to education.

The influence of the Broad Church movement upon the social life of England was important. By helping the workingmen find a solution for their religious doubts, and by demonstrating that the church had an interest in their welfare, it was able to retain many of them for Christianity. It also infused into the institutions of Owen the inspiration of a religious altruism,[2] and by infecting the spirit that propagated socialism with "a deep distrust for either sharply cut class lines or of intensely dogmatic positions",[2] it greatly hindered the development of a strong socialistic party in England. Its value here is, of course, an open question. To the Chartist movement after 1848 it contributed indirectly by (1) bringing to the classes of England a better understanding of one another, and (2) by preparing through education the English workingman for an eventual successful attainment of his desires.

II. THE WESLEYAN METHODIST CHURCH AND ITS OFFSHOOTS

The fact that the Established Church took up a position bitterly opposed to Chartism, can surprise no one. It might

[1] *Life of Maurice*, vol. ii, p. 40.
[2] Hall, *op. cit.*, p. 204.

be supposed, however, that the Methodists, if not actually
coöperating with the Chartists, would at least be in sympathy with them, and this for several reasons. In the first
place, speaking broadly, Methodism was the religion of the
poorer classes,[1] as Chartism was their politics. " Methodism," said Lecky, " has long since taken its position as preeminently and almost exclusively the religion of the middle
and lower classes of society." [2] The great majority of
Wesleyan preachers were recruited from the poorer people,
from the promising local preachers who, with their intelli-
gence and antecedents, might be expected to support any
scheme for the political or social advancement of the people.
Again, Methodism won its greatest successes amongst the
operatives and miners,[3] the classes particularly favorable
to Chartism. Finally, even the enemies of Methodism and
Chartism were the same, namely, that " hereditary wealth
and influence, whether landed, manufacturing or mercan-
tile." [4] Why was it, then, that Methodism, at least the official
Methodism of the largest branch, the Wesleyan Methodists,
assumed an attitude so uncompromising in opposition to the
democratic innovations of the Chartists? To answer this
question it is worth while to run back briefly over the connexional history and general political outlook of the Methodists.

The Wesleyan Methodist Church, as it developed, assumed
the form of a " connexion," which has been defined as " a
number of societies who have agreed to unite themselves
in a common bond of doctrine and discipline, under a com-

[1] *Minutes,* vol. x, p. 102.

[2] Lecky, *England in the Eighteenth Century,* vol. ii, p. 640.

[3] *Quarterly Review,* no. 139, p. 167.

[4] Rigg, *The Connexional Economy of Wesleyan Meth.* (London,
1879), pp. 201, 202.

mon code of regulations and usages, and under a common government."[1] This sounds harmless enough; but in the form it took under Wesley and his successors it resembled far more the closely-knit organization of the Episcopal and Catholic than that of the Independent and other nonconformist churches of England. Over the classes, societies, circuits and districts were appointed teachers, lay preachers, ministers, superintendents, and over these the conference and *Legal Hundred*,[2] " oversight, as in the Society of Jesus, being reduced to an exact science."[3] Power was almost exclusively in the hands of the ministers, the control of the laymen being almost a minus quantity. As a natural consequence, the history of Wesleyan Methodism since the death of Wesley has been largely a record of revolts and attempts to introduce more democracy into the government of the church.

While Wesley lived he was able to exercise a paternal absolutism through the force of his superior personality and intellectual gifts and through his position as the founder of a new movement. But the control which he possessed as father of the movement did not rest so gracefully on the shoulders of his legal successors, the Hundred Ministers, and troubles were not long coming. In 1795 Kilham, not satisfied with the reforms of the " Plan of Pacification," published his pamphlet, *The Progress of Liberty Among the People Called Methodists*, was expelled, and started the Methodist New Connexion. In 1806 the " Band Room Methodists " broke away, and in 1810 Bourne and

[1] Watson, *An Affectionate Address*, p. 4.

[2] By a Deed of Declaration in the Court of Chancery, February 28, 1784, Wesley passed on his power at his death to a conference of one hundred ministers, in whom was vested the full government of the Wesleyan Methodists.

[3] Faulkner, in *New International Encyclopædia*, 2d ed., vol. xv, p. 505.

his companions, having been expelled during the camp-meeting controversy,[1] started the Primitive Methodists—a body of earnest followers of Wesley, who have increased largely in the nineteenth century. O'Bryan in 1815, after his expulsion, organized his societies into what were later called Bible Christians. In 1828 the Leeds Organ case; in 1834 the expulsion of J. R. Stephens; in 1835 the Warren controversy and the affair of the Rochdale petitioners; and in 1836 the secession of the Arminian Methodists, caused considerable loss and some few concessions. When in 1849 even free speech became impossible under Bunting and his followers, the most important agitation of all, that of Everett, Dunn and Griffith, resulted in a membership loss of 100,000 and a revenue loss of £100,000 in three years.

Concerning these secessions two facts stand forth preeminently. In the first place, all of them, with one minor exception (that of the Arminians in 1835), were on political and administrative, not doctrinal grounds, and caused by dissatisfaction with the form of government. Secondly, the agitations in the church were closely associated in point of time with periods of political and revolutionary agitation in England and Europe. The Methodist agitations were grouped around three periods: first, the period of the French Revolution when the followers of Kilham broke away; second, the period of the agitation for the Reform Bill when the Leeds Organ case and the Warren affair disturbed the church; and third, the revolutionary period of 1848 which resulted in the Wesleyan Reform Movement. " The revolutionary ideas of the Chartist Period (1840-1848) and of Continental politics (1848-1849) reacted

---

[1] *Minutes* for 1807 and 1810.

upon Wesleyan Methodism as the political ideas of 1791 and 1831 had done in these epochs." [1]

Along with this distrust of democracy in church government there was a distinctly conservative policy in political matters. This was inherited from Wesley himself, who, as a Tory, always stood for the *status quo* in government and for the powers that be, his writings apparently lacking any sympathy for popular government.[2] In the rules of 1797 the Wesleyan Methodists put themselves on official record with the following: " None of us shall, either in writing or conversation, speak lightly or irreverently of the government under which we live. The oracles of God command us to be subject to the higher powers; and ' honour the King ' is there connected with the fear of God." A similar tone is evinced elsewhere.[3]   If we are to believe official promulgations, the Methodists avoided assiduously any political affiliations.   Number twelve of the *Liverpool Minutes of 1820* seeks to impress upon the people that they "do not exist for purposes of party." [4]   The conference never tires of impressing upon the ministers and people that their business is not of this world and demanding that they keep themselves apart from political agitation.[5]   The problem was fought out and decided, at least to the satisfaction of those in authority, in 1834, when J. R. Stephens, later famous in the Chartist movement, was suspended from the

---

[1] J. H. Rigg, in *Enc. Brit.*, 9th ed., vol. xvi, p. 198.

[2] See his pamphlets, "Thoughts on Liberty," *Works*, vol. xi, pp. 34-46; "Free Thoughts on Public Affairs," vol. xi, pp. 14-34; "Thoughts Concerning the Origin of Power," vol. xi, pp. 46-53; and J. A. Faulkner's "Socialism of John Wesley," in *Social Tracts for the Times*.

[3] *Minutes*, vol. ii, p. 61; vol. iii, p. 303; vol. viii, pp. 236, 247, 371; vol. ix, p. 119, *etc.*

[4] *Minutes* of 1820; Williams, *The Constitution and Polity of Wesleyan Methodism* (London, 1880), appendix iii.

[5] *Minutes*, vol. viii, pp. 105, 237, 242; vol. x, p. 260.

connexion for actively associating himself with the movement in favor of separation of church and state.[1]   At this time it was officially enunciated again that " Methodism does not exist for the purpose of party," and that " a Wesleyan minister who takes a prominent political position and occupies his time and thought in furthering the ' purposes of party ' acts ' contrary to his peculiar calling and solemn engagements as a Methodist preacher '." [2]   This policy was carried so far that the Wesleyan Methodists were the only dissenting church which would not coöperate in the Anti-Corn Law agitation.[3]

With such conservative antecedents it was hardly likely that the Chartist movement would be very popular with the controlling element of Wesleyan Methodism.   The reasons may be collected under three heads:

I. Chartism was a democratic movement.   From a church whose whole previous ecclesiastical existence had been largely devoted to the hopeless task of fighting off democratic innovation, Chartism could hope for little favor.   Those in the church, like Griffith, who were sympathetic toward Chartism, were also in favor of a more popular administration in church government.   This in itself was enough to condemn Chartism with those in power.   " Methodism," Jabez Bunting is reputed to have said, " hates democracy as much as it hates sin," [4] and its foes were not reticent in

[1] *Minutes*, vol. vii, pp. 417 *et seq.*, 436; Gregory, *Handbook*, pp. 200 *et seq.*

[2] In actual practice, however, they did not hesitate to interfere in secular politics when their interests appeared to be endangered. *Vide New History of Methodism*, vol. i, pp. 402, 416; Pierce, *The Ecclesiastical Principles and Polity of the Wesleyan Methodists*, 3d ed. (London, 1873), pp. 498 *et seq.; Minutes*, vol. ii, p. 185.

[3] Prentice, *History of the Anti-Corn Law League*, vol. i, pp. 233, 234.

[4] *Methodism as It Is*, p. ii.

dwelling on this point.[1] Several historians have recognized this conservatism of the Methodists [2] and have testified to its becalming influence upon political life, Taine going so far as to claim that it saved England from a revolution similar to the French.[3] This policy they were determined to continue.

II. Periods of political agitation had heretofore proved themselves detrimental to the propagation of the Gospel and to the welfare of the connexion.[4] In the opinion of the Wesleyan Methodists political agitation led " to the wreck of all piety." [5] During the Chartist period emigration was very heavy and seriously depleted the ranks of the Wesleyans.[6] The years 1837, 1842, 1848 and 1852 showed actual decreases in membership, although the total period from 1838-1848 gave an increase.[7] The Primitive Methodists, however, a branch democratically administered, more than doubled their membership during the Chartist period.[8] The great agitations within the church, as has been pointed out, ran parallel with the democratic movements in secular policies, and the most serious of all with the Chartist movement, which undoubtedly influenced it. The Chartist churches also drew from Wesleyan Methodist membership.

[1] *Supra*, p. 22; *Jubilee of the Methodist New Connexion* (London, 1848), p. 384.

[2] Lecky, *op. cit.*, vol. ii, p. 637.

[3] *New History of Methodism*, vol. i, pp. 362, 371.

[4] Avery, *Memorials of Rev. John Henley* (London, 1844), p. 389; Beech, *The Good Soldier* (London, 1848), p. 93.

[5] *Minutes*, vol. iv, p. 414; vol. x, p. 560.

[6] *Minutes*, vol. viii, p. 308; vol. ix, pp. 114, 257, 268, 420, 427, 564, 575; vol. ix, pp. 128, 132, 310, 500.

[7] In 1838 there were 296,800; in 1848, 338,860.

[8] For 1833 there were 48,421; in 1850, 104,710.

III. The attitude of the Chartists in regard to ecclesiastical and religious matters was unacceptable. If the democracy of Chartism was to be condemned how much more was its religious heterodoxy![1] The infidelity associated with the movement[2] was made much of,[3] while its good works went unnoticed. The doctrine of separation of church and state,[4] which was an actual platform of the Convention of 1851[5] and a generally accepted belief among the Chartists, was not in much favor among the Wesleyans. The latter were rather " in favor of its being maintained,"[6] regarding the Establishment " as one of the main bulwarks of the Protestant faith."[7] The fate of Stephens, when he implicated the Methodists in the dispute, has been recounted.[8] Furthermore the humor of such a typical Chartist battlecry as " More pigs and fewer parsons "[9] appealed as little to the Methodists[10] as to the Anglicans.

The official pronouncements of the Wesleyan Methodists on the Chartist movement are to be found in the yearly pastoral letters to the people, signed by the president and secretary of the conference. Although Chartism as such is not mentioned by name the implications are unmistakable. In these letters the Methodists are repeatedly urged to keep

[1] Solly, *James Woodford*, vol. ii, p. 9.
[2] *Supra*, pp. 14 *et seq.*
[3] *Minutes*, vol. ix, pp. 115, 125, 403, 410; vol. x, 112, 127, 137; *Wes. Meth. Mag.*, 3d series, vol. xvii, p. 153.
[4] *Supra*, pp. 34 *et seq.*
[5] Gammage, *op. cit.*, p. 371.
[6] Bunting, *Life of Jabez Bunting* (London, 1878), p. 289.
[7] *Minutes*, vol. iv, p. 557.
[8] *Supra*, p. 18.
[9] *Anti-Socialist Gazette*, Dec. 1841, p. 36.
[10] Gregory, *Sidelights of the Conflicts of Methodism* (London, 1898), p. 344.

out of political agitations,[1] to remain loyal to the throne.[2] to beware of democratic innovators (who are, of course, infidels)[3] and are assured that the " only effectual remedy for the ills and sufferings of our fallen world and our unhappy country is to be found in the glorious gospel of the blessed God." [4] While much concerned over the fact that " Some portions of our laboring population have been intoxicated and deluded by the ravings of lawless democrats," [5] and " disloyal and disaffected men have been endeavoring to allure the humbler classes of our fellow-countrymen to take part in their schemes," the writers yet have received " unspeakable pleasure " [6] in the attachment to the throne and constitution which their followers have evinced.

The platform of the *Wesleyan Methodist Magazine*, the official organ of the church under the editorship of Thomas Jackson (1839-41) and George Cubitt (1842-50), corresponded on social questions closely to that of the ruling powers, as laid down in the letters. The same concern over such questions as slavery and Catholicism, and the same lack of comprehension and understanding of the more serious evils close at hand are seen here as in the minutes.[7] The same inability or disinclination to discriminate between democracy and infidelity and the same distrust of democracy are apparent. While its policy was to " conscientiously

[1] *Minutes*, vol. viii, pp. 96, 105, 237; vol. ix, pp. 414; vol. x, p. 566.
[2] *Minutes*, vol. viii, pp. 247, 272, 371; vol. xi, p. 119.
[3] *Minutes*, vol. ix, pp. 115, 403.
[4] *Minutes*, vol. xi, p. 501.
[5] *Minutes*, vol. ix, p. 125.
[6] *Minutes*, vol. xi, p. 119.
[7] Third series, vol. xvii, p. 153. Also vol. xix, p. 955; vol. xix. headings under Socialism; vol. xxiii, p. 155.

stand aloof from all politics "[1] yet an expression of opinion would inadvertently crop out.[2] Convinced that " Infidelity and democracy convert human beings into fiends ",[3] the *Wesleyan Methodist Magazine* offers Christian education as a cure, for

A people thoroughly educated on Christian principles can neither be the slave of a despot, nor the tools or puppets of some arbitrary government, on the one hand; nor can they be restless, dissatisfied murmurers, insurrectionary anarchists, the instruments by which the political adventurers seek to gain power, whom he flatters and despises, and on whom, finally, in the hour of triumph he tramples.[4]

The traditional policy of the Wesleyan Methodists was loyally upheld by those who controlled their destinies during these years. Such men as Jabez Bunting,[5] John Beecham,[6] James Dixon,[7] George Cubitt, Joseph Fowler,[8] John Hannah,[9] Thomas Jackson,[10] Robert Newton,[11] and F. J. Jobson[12] could find nothing to favor in Chartism.

The preceding discussion, it should be borne in mind, has reference only to the Wesleyan Methodist Church and not to its numerous offshoots. These branches, as we have seen, developed primarily because they could not fit in with

---

[1] *Wes. Meth. Mag.*, 4th series, vol. iv, p. 463.

[2] *Ibid.*, vol. xviii, pp. 41, 313.   [3] *Ibid.*, vol. xvii, pp. 153, 295.

[4] Fourth series, vol. i, March, 1845, in " Christian Retrospect."

[5] Jobson, *A Tribute*, pp. 70, 71 ; Bunting, *Life of Bunting*, vol. ii, p. 291.

[6] *Methodism as It Is*, vol. ii, p. 881.

[7] Gregory, *op. cit.*, p. 197; Dixon, *Life of James Dixon*, pp. 214, 222, 225, 230.

[8] Gregory, *op. cit.*, p. 328; *Minutes*, vol. xi, p. 118.

[9] Jobson, *The Beloved Disciple*, p. 107; *Minutes*, vol. ix, p. 125.

[10] *Minutes*, vol. viii, p. 37; *Wes. Meth. Mag.*, vol. xix, p. 955.

[11] Pastoral Letters for 1840 and 1842.

[12] Hurst, *History of Methodism*, vol. iii, p. 1360.

the conservative constitutional policy of the older church. An expanding democracy in the state demanded its counterpart in the church, and the result is seen in the attitude of such branches as the Primitive Methodists and the Methodist New Connexion. In a semi-official publication the latter church is found standing for " representation of all interests, freedom of commerce, voluntary support of religion, liberty of thought, enlightened piety, Christian union, and strong solicitude for the welfare of the masses in humble life." [1] Perhaps the most noted of the ministers of the Methodist offshoots who became actively associated with the Chartist movement was James Scholefield, Bible Christian, of Manchester. In an attempt to break up an Anti-Corn Law meeting held in Manchester, March 19, 1841, he was nominated by the Chartists as chairman, but, as it was claimed that the mayor of the city also received the show of hands, both had desks on the platform.[2] A couple of years later a Chartist conference of factory operatives was held in his chapel, and he was among those tried at the Lancaster assizes of March, 1843 for sedition and incitation to riot, but found not guilty.[3]

Furthermore, while the foregoing statements have been true of official Methodism and of an overwhelming majority of its ministers, there was undoubtedly in the rank and file a more liberal spirit pervading. The numerous agitations are a striking proof of the continued dissatisfaction. The radicals, while they condemned the ruling powers in the Methodist church, were free to admit that aid might be expected from the ranks, if the people were only free agents.

[1] *Jubilee of the Methodist New Connexion*, pp. 386, 387. See also p. 384.

[2] Prentice, *History of the Anti-Corn Law League*, vol. i, p. 184.

[3] Gammage *op. cit.*, pp. 232, 235, 427.

Thus Archibald Prentice, Chartist and free-trader, said that many Wesleyans " were willing to give their aid in promoting cheapness and plenty " but for the hostile influence of the leaders.[1] The *Eclectic Review* [2] goes so far as to say that

Had the people who compose the body free scope for the manifestation of their sentiments, we cannot doubt that the influence of Wesleyanism would be freely given to all measures for the reform of abuses, for the improvement of the physical and moral condition of the community, and for the abolition of every law and every institution which interferes with the fullest extension of our civil and religious liberties. But tied down as the Wesleyans are by laws which prevent them from moving hand or foot, and by usages which beget a servile spirit, the country and the legislature must receive their notions of the state of opinions in the Wesleyan church from the conference and its commissions. Nor can we expect that those who have tried to build ever upon the foundation of this voluntary principle, so compact a structure of priestly authority in their own favor, will ever exert their political influence in support of any line of state policy, which might afterwards be quoted as a precedent for the entire submission of this lordly hierarchy.

During the Chartist period Methodist discontent with the despotic administration of Bunting and his followers grew apace. Finally, in 1849, upon the expulsion of Everett, Dunn and Griffith, an agitation was started which in its form and procedure was remarkably similar to that of Chartism, even to the phraseology of its war-cries. One of the demands was for " The Bible, the Whole Bible and nothing but the Bible ". These demands in the form of a petition were called " The People's Declaration " [3] Such

---

[1] Prentice, *op. cit.*, vol. i, pp. 233, 234.

[2] August, 1846, article " Methodism as It Is."

[3] *Wesleyan Vindicator*, p. 120.

methods of arousing the people were evidently successful, for the followers of Bunting and the old system were strong in their denunciation of them. The following quotation will show how strikingly the method resembled that of the Chartists.

To succeed in this attempt [said the *Wesleyan Vindicator*], Christian agitators resorted to the most unchristian means. Public meetings were called, composed of all classes of the British community. Not only deluded Methodists, but worldly politicians, and notoriously ungodly men and women were appealed to for judgment on Wesleyan rule and government. Calumny, slander, and reviling, were poured forth in concert upon the most eminent and beloved ministers. A monster Petition and " Bill of Rights " as it was called was hawked about in parts, which were afterwards to be put together, and to astonish the Connexion by the vast amount of signatures it should have secured. Secret pledges were received to " stand or fall " by the leading agitators, and their plans for Wesleyan Reform; and the meetings held by pretended Delegates to discuss the questions at issue and to secure the appointment of "A Committee of Privileges for the People " to care for their rights and liberties.[1]

The reformers were accused of associating with themselves dissenters and political agitators of all kinds,[2] including Chartists, and there is every reason to believe the accusation was true. " Red Republicans " and " Chartists " were frequent epithets [3] used by the discomfited members of the old church to describe their seceding brethren. Additional force was given to the accusation by the fact that William Griffith, one of the three leaders in the Wesleyan Reform agitation, " was politically a radical of the most

[1] *Wesleyan Vindicator*, p. 207.
[2] *Ibid.*, p. 21.   [3] *Ibid.*, pp. 30, 67, 86.

extreme type, and took no pains to conceal his principles." [1]
During the agitation he was continually referred to as a
Chartist but so far from resenting this he apparently gloried
in it. " If I am a Chartist," he said,[2] " I got my principles
from the Bible. That book is my political pocket-book. I
hold no opinions but what I find in the book of God." In
another place [3] he expresses himself as follows: "As long
as I believe in the Bible, a Chartist of that school I will be,
and I will teach the workingman to think that he is a man
and that it is his own fault if he is not as noble, as respectable as any man who walks the face of the earth." " His
political opinions," he said, " were all drawn from the
Bible, and he must have a new Bible before he could have a
new political creed." [4]

If the attitude of Wesleyan Methodism toward political
matters was conservative no such charge can be brought
forward in regard to its philanthropy. The great out-
burst of philanthropy which accompanied the origin of
Methodism [5] had enough vitality to extend itself partially
through the so-called " middle period " of the church. This
benevolence, combined with a religious generosity in regard
to tenets of salvation [6]—regarding all who loved God as the
elect,—put enough heart into the followers of Wesley to
effect some practical results which influenced indirectly their
political life. The most notable of this philanthropic work
must be reckoned the activity of the Methodists in factory
reform. Richard Oastler, Michael Thomas Sadler and
Rev. J. R. Stephens, the men who made factory reform a

[1] Bunting, *Life of Jabez Bunting*, vol. ii, p. 346.
[2] *Methodism as It Is*, vol. ii, p. 415.
[3] *Ibid.*, vol. ii, pp. 241, 242.
[4] *Ibid.*, vol. ii, p. 343.
[5] North, *Early Methodist Philanthropy* (New York, 1914).
[6] Holyoake, *Life of J. R. Stephens* (London, 1881), p. 78.

great cause, were all nurtured in the Methodist Church.[1] The agitation for the ten-hour bill and factory reform, which these three instituted, was a distinct contributing force to the organization of the Chartist movement,[2] as was also the opposition to the New Poor Law which found its mouthpiece in Stephens and Oastler.[3]

It was only a step from the opposition to the New Poor Law to Chartism, and, although Stephens reiterated that he was no Chartist,[4] he was a frequent speaker at Chartist meetings. At Kersall Moor he seconded a resolution in favor of the Charter and he was elected a representative from Ashton to the Convention of 1839 [5] which he attended.[6] He gave momentary adherence to the Charter because no other course seemed open whereby the people could be helped.[7] Tory as he was, his Toryism was of that brand which considered the welfare of the people the most important issue.[8] The earnestness with which he believed this often led him into the most extravagant and inflammatory language, entirely unrestrained by prudence. Incitement to the use of arms was the distinguishing burden of many of his orations.[9] Arrested on December 27, 1838, on three separate charges of attending illegal meetings and using

[1] Holyoake, *op. cit.*, pp. 78 *et seq.*

[2] Tildsley, *Die Entstehung und die ökonomischen Grundsätze der Chartistenbewegung*, pp. 16 *et seq.*

[3] *Ibid.*, p. 28.

[4] Holyoake, *Life of J. R. Stephens*, pp. 146, 155, 171; Lovett, *op. cit.*, p. 195.

[5] Gammage, *op. cit.*, pp. 57, 59, 61, 62, 92, 96.

[6] Lovett, *op. cit.*, p. 207; Holyoake, *op. cit.*, p. 143.

[7] Holyoake, *op. cit.*, p. 232.

[8] *Ibid.*, pp. 18 *et seq.*

[9] Gammage, *op. cit.*, pp. 56, 95; Lovett, *op. cit.*, p. 291.

seditious language,[1] he was sentenced in August, 1839, to eighteen months' imprisonment, thus having the " honour of being the first man on whom the government sought to wreak the vengeance of the law " [2] for participation in the Chartist movement. One of the best known and popular leaders at the time of his arrest, he severed himself from Chartism [3] upon his release but remained throughout his life active in social work.

Other prominent Chartists also had their first religious affiliation with the Methodists. Lovett's mother was a most devoted Methodist,[4] while he for a while belonged to the Bryanites or Bible Christians.[5] Thomas Cooper had acted as a local preacher for the Methodists in Lincoln but was suspended for protesting at the appointment of a super-intendent,[6] voluntarily resigned from the connection and soon drifted into free thought. Joseph Barker, another erratic genius prominent in Chartism, started with the Meth-odists.[7] Educated at Methodist schools, he served his ap-prenticeship with them as a local preacher but forsook the Wesleyans for the Methodist New Connexion. From this branch he was expelled in 1841 for denying the divine ap-pointment of baptism. With him seceded twenty-nine churches and 4,348 members.[8] He likewise soon drifted to free-thought, but after a stormy career as a political and religious radical he returned to Christianity.[9]

[1] Gammage, *op. cit.*, p. 48.

[2] *Ibid.*, pp. 99, 100.

[3] Holyoake, *op. cit.*, p. 228.

[4] Lovett, *op. cit.*, p. 7.

[5] *Ibid.*, p. 22.

[6] Cooper, *Life of Thomas Cooper*, pp. 101, 102.

[7] *Dictionary of National Biography*, vol. iii, p. 205.

[8] *New History of Methodism*, vol. i, p. 525.

[9] Barker, *Modern Skepticism: a Life Story, passim*.

III. THE OTHER NONCONFORMIST CHURCHES

Although the membership of the other Nonconformist churches was recruited largely from the bourgeoisie, there was, broadly speaking, among both pastor and people of these denominations a more tolerant attitude toward a further extension of the franchise than that evinced by either the State Church or the Wesleyan Methodists. The committee appointed to organize the Complete Suffrage Movement and call the conference reported a constantly growing class, " which included many ministers of religion ", of those who had

long been dissatisfied with the manifest injustice of any system of representation that excluded the majority from all share in their own government, but who have hitherto kept aloof from taking any active share in public affairs, partly because they wish to avoid the strife of men and tongues and partly because no practical remedy had yet been offered which there appeared much chance of attaining.[1]

The committee further reported that " Nearly, if not more than two hundred ministers of religion, of almost all denominations, have signed the declaration or memorial ", and continued with an optimism hardly warranted, " there is every reason to believe that the greater number of those not endowed by the state will do so when called on." [2]

While the coöperation of so many dissenting ministers in the holding of a Complete Suffrage Conference was one of the most significant facts in the whole problem of the relationship between the Chartist movement and the church, it should not be overestimated. The signing of the memorial did not bind them to endorse the proceedings of the conference nor did it make Chartists of them. Complete

[1] *Proceedings of the Conference*, p. 5.　　[2] *Ibid.*, p. 7.

suffrage was, while the most important, only one of the
Six Points. The state of mind of the average dissenting
minister, liberally inclined, was nowhere better expressed
than in a speech delivered by the Rev. Andrew Marshall
in Edinburgh on December 16, 1840, and later published
as an *Address to the Dissenting Ministers of Scotland*
(United Secession Synod). The working classes, said
Marshall, have long since been alienated from the State
Church and have long regarded its clergy as their enemies.
They are now coming to look upon the dissenting ministers
in the same light. It is the duty of the latter, as the best
qualified, to stem the current and save the masses to the
church and to morality, peace and order. The only way
that this can be done is to show some sympathy toward their
efforts for an extended franchise. This the ministers
should do, not by political agitation for the Charter
nor by making speeches or holding meetings, but simply
by avowing " on all proper occasions " that they were " in
favor of a more extended suffrage " [1] As to the Chartists,
he condemns their methods and states that there are probably few dissenting ministers anywhere more obnoxious to
them than himself, several having left his church because
of his attitude.[2] This speech when delivered caused great
excitement in the meeting and the interruptions were so
frequent that Marshall had to stop before he had finished
it.[3] It expressed, nevertheless, the prevailing sentiment
of those ministers who signed the Complete Suffrage Memorial. The Nonconformist ministers, as they were for
the most part responsible only to their own congregations,
were often in a position to enter actively into political agi-

[1] Marshall, *The Duty of Attempting to Reconcile the Unenfranchised
with the Enfranchised Classes*, p. 14.

[2] *Ibid.*, p. 10.

[3] *Ibid.*, p. 15.

tation if they could carry a majority of their people with
them, and some felt themselves in duty bound to do so.

The difference between the political attitude of the leaders
of Wesleyan Methodism and of Congregationalism was not
very great. Although it is true that several Congregationalists participated in the Anti-Corn Law Conference,[1] but
few of the leaders, especially those in London, would entertain for a moment the idea of the denomination, as such,
concerning itself in political matters. This feeling was
carried to the extent that even in the matter of the separation of church and state any active political agitation was
firmly opposed by such men as Conder and Vaughan, who
were able to obtain the support of the *Congregational Magazine* and the official promulgations of the Congregational
Union.[2]

The conservatism of the majority and of the London
leaders, however, was decidedly distasteful to a small but
active and growing minority in the provinces. Unable
longer to keep silence under what was considered " the be-
trayal of their sacred trust ",[3] this group, with the aid of
the advocates of voluntaryism of all denominations, determined upon the establishment of a weekly newspaper in
London, " having for its aim the faithful and persistent
exposition of the principles of civil and religious liberty." [4]
Consequently, on April 14, 1841, the first issue of the *Nonconformist* appeared under the editorship of Edward Miall,
who quickly developed into one of the most brilliant jour-
nalists of the time. Although proposed principally to give
voice to the Disestablishment movement, the *Nonconform-*

[1] Waddington, *Congregational History, Continuation to 1850*, pp. 557
et seq.

[2] *Ibid.*, pp. 548, 551, 553 *et seq.*, 572, 574 *et seq.*

[3] *Ibid.*, p. 551.

[4] Miall, *Life of Edward Miall*, p. 38.

ist soon became the exponent of liberalism on all lines. The
question of the suffrage was taken up with characteristic
vigor in a series of editorials, the influence of which was so
great that it became the official organ of the National Complete Suffrage Union.[1] Its success was immediate, its circulation jumping from a few hundreds to two thousand at the
end of the first year,[2] showing that the radicalism of Miall
was far from offensive to many Nonconformists. Although
warmly welcomed and frequently quoted by the Chartist
press and by liberal papers of all shades of opinion, it en-
countered great opposition in religious circles. " The
authorities were clearly against it," said Miall, while " all
mention of it was studiously avoided in those periodical
publications which Dissenters are wont to consult." [3] Naturally it was not long before the *Nonconformist* met direct opposition from the *Congregational Magazine*[4] and the powers
in the church.[5] Fortunately Miall found an ally in the
Eclectic Review, edited by Dr. Price, which, while not
going so far in its political views as the *Nonconformist,*
yet put itself unhesitatingly on the side of both political and
religious reforms.[6] The aim of Dr. Price was " to win the
mass of the people by advocating their cause in relation to
political rights." [7]

To counteract the influence of the *Eclectic,* Vaughan and
his associates of the conservative Congregational school decided a new periodical was necessary, and the *British Quarterly Review* was the result.[8] The number of Congrega-

[1] Miall, *Life of Edward Miall,* p. 87. See *infra,* p. 113.
[2] *Ibid.,* p. 54.
[3] *Ibid.,* p. 54.
[4] Waddington, *op. cit.,* p. 572.   [5] *Ibid.,* p. 553.
[6] April, 1843.
[7] Waddington, *op. cit.,* p. 578.
[8] *Ibid.,* pp. 557, 578.

tional journals was also augmented all this time by Dr. John Campbell (1795-1867) who was in turn editor of the *Christian Witness*, the *Christian Penny Magazine*, and the *British Banner*. Campbell was inclined to take a middle course. While believing that there was no great discontent in the country,[1] he was yet willing to advocate a reformation of the House of Lords and triennial parliaments. Universal suffrage, however, was entirely out of the question; the utmost that could " rationally be expected, or prudently desired ", said he, " is Household Suffrage." [2]

In this manner each type of political thought had representatives upon the Congregational press. While the conservatives were decidedly predominant in official circles, the radicalism of the Miall school was slowly forcing its way to the front and was destined in later years to affect greatly the policies of the denomination.

Of all the Nonconformist denominations, with the possible exception of the Unitarians, the Baptists probably showed the most sympathy toward the democratic schemes of the Chartists. This was partially due to the fact that the whole tone of the church was more radical than that, for instance, of the Congregational. This was excellently illustrated during the effort for the separation of church and state. While only a small advanced party of Congregationalists were in favor of an active political campaign for this reform, an overwhelming majority of Baptists were committed to it. At the Conference of the Liberation Society in 1844 the Baptists were the only denomination to send delegates.[3] In a similar manner the *Eclectic Review*,

---

[1] *Reformer's Almanac*, p. 200.

[2] *Ibid.*, p. 205.

[3] Carlile, *Story of the English Baptists*, p. 227.

a liberal paper favorable to an increase in the suffrage,[1] was the literary periodical of only the radical wing of the Congregationalists, but of the great majority of the Baptists.

Still more radical than the *Eclectic Review* were the *Nonconformist*, largely supported by the Baptists, and the *Church Baptist Penny Magazine* founded in 1848.[2] The liberal influence of these papers was greatly augmented by the well-known advanced political views of many of the leading ministers of the denomination. Among these men were George Dawson,[3] one of the most famous of nineteenth-century English preachers; J. P. Mursell,[4] prominent in the Complete Suffrage Conference; Eustace Giles, one of the founders of the *Baptist Union* and one of the best friends the Chartists had amongst the middle class; John Jenkinson of Kettering, active in Chartism;[5] and William Jackson of Manchester, who was sentenced to eighteen months imprisonment for "maliciously conspiring and inciting the people of this country to make riots, to arm with weapons of offense, and with divers other acts for the promotion of rebellion."[6] The Baptists were also fortunate in having at their head such men as Dr. Steane who were willing to take the lead in social reform.

Carlile, a leading Baptist historian, goes so far as to say that the sympathies of the Baptists for Chartism were expressed by Thomas Cooper.[7] Although this is an exag-

[1] *Minutes of the Proceedings of the Conference of Representatives of the Middle and Working Classes*, p. 7; *Eclectic Magazine*, April, 1843.

[2] *The Republican*, p. 40, favorably reviews it, saying "that its political tendency is toward Democracy."

[3] Afterwards left the Baptists and started an independent church.

[4] *English Chartist Circular*, p. 181.

[5] Gammage, *op. cit.*, p. 37.

[6] *Ibid.*, pp. 178, 179; also 152.

[7] Carlile, *Story of the English Baptists*, pp. 224, 225.

geration, there is no doubt that Chartist principles made considerable headway in the denomination. O'Neill obtained a large part of the membership of his Christian Chartist Church from the Baptists,[1] and Disraeli in his Chartist novel makes one of the inner circle of conspirators a Baptist teacher.[2] It is also interesting to note that two of the leading Chartist agitators, Cooper [3] and O'Neill,[4] later became ministers in that denomination, as did also Charles Vince.[5]

In proportion to their membership the Quakers had undoubtedly surpassed all denominations of English Christians in their philanthropy. The names of Joseph Lancaster and William Allen in education, Clarkson and Gurney in the anti-slavery movement, and Elizabeth Fry in prison reform, are sufficient to indicate in a slight degree this fact. It was not a mere accident that four of the six partners whom Owen associated with himself in the New Lanark scheme in 1813 were Quakers.[6]

The emphasis upon benevolence was encouraged in the official promulgations of the society, issued at the Yearly Meetings in London [7] which are filled with wholesome advice upon all sorts of subjects including the conduct of business. In these epistles the society does not hesitate to state boldly its detestation of war,[8] of the slave

[1] Solly, *James Woodford*, vol. ii, p. 90.

[2] Disraeli, *Sybil*, p. 375.

[3] Cooper, *Life of Cooper*, pp. 380, 381.

[4] Gammage, *History of the Chartist Movement*, p. 402.

[5] Richard, *Memoirs of Sturge*, p. 328.

[6] Podmore, *Life of Owen*, vol. i, p. 97. Owen, however, accuses Allen, one of the four, of secretly trying to undermine his views and authority. Owen's *Life*, vol. i, p. 141.

[7] *Christian Discipline*, pp. 125-130.

[8] *Ibid.*, pp. 153, 158.

trade,[1] of oaths, and of tithes and all ecclesiastical assumption,[2] yet desires it to be known that the Quakers, where conscience is not infringed, are anxious to be considered amongst the " quiet in the land " and in full subjection to the civil government.[3] While ambitious that the members should coöperate in every benevolent scheme, the epistles are in great fear lest these endeavors may involve them in party politics which endanger the virtues they hold dear [4] and have a tendency to lead them " away from that patient exercise of spirit and that quiet self-examination, which are not only conducive but necessary to a growth in grace." [5]

Notwithstanding the frequent warnings of the Yearly Meetings many Quakers felt it their duty actively and strenuously to enter the arena of party politics in behalf of the Factory Acts and in opposition to the Corn Laws.[6] It was not at all illogical, then, that when the attempt was made to reconcile the middle and lower classes on a basis of complete suffrage, Joseph Sturge, the most noted philanthropist of his time and a Quaker, should be chosen almost by tacit consent to lead the movement. The honesty of his motives was too obvious to be questioned by either Chartist or Tory, while the unselfishness with which he had previously coöperated in philanthropic labors assured for any scheme which he might advocate at least a hearing from all parties.[7] With the same enthusiasm he had shown

1 *Christian Discipline*, pp. 159-163.   2 *Ibid.*, pp. 137 *et seq.*
3 *Ibid.*, pp. 132 *et seq.*   4 *Epistles*, vol. ii, p. 303.
5 *Ibid.*, vol. ii, p. 314; also vol. ii, pp. 301, 332.
6 Emmott, *The Story of Quakerism*, p. 179.
7 " In such case your name is the very best in all England to head the list. I say this without compliment, or even views of doing you justice, but simply with an eye to policy. You have so much of established reputation to fall back upon that your standing with the middle class would not be endangered by a course which might peril the character and endanger the usefulness of most others. You should carry with

in the emancipation agitation, Sturge threw himself into the activities of the Complete Suffrage Union, notwithstanding the fact that this political move was observed with sorrow and disapproval by many members of his own religious society.[1] Among the delegates at the Complete Suffrage Conference was the Quaker, John Bright, destined to do even more than Sturge in the cause of democracy. Among the Chartists, Vincent seems to be the only one of prominence who inclined toward the Quakers,[2] although George Binns was of Quaker parentage.[3]

The bugbear of Catholicism was ever present in the minds of Englishmen during the first half of the century.[4] Politicians had but to raise the cry of papal aggression, and Churchmen and Dissenters would both for the time being forget their differences in the face of this greater danger. It was consequently to be expected that in the heat of recrimination some one would endeavor to prove a connection between the Chartist movement and Catholicism. It so turned out and the charge was not infrequently made. It had a touch of plausibility about it because several of the leaders, like O'Connor and O'Brien, were Irishmen. Even O'Connell in the early days of Chartism had professed to give it his support.[5] But O'Connell soon changed his stand and became a bitter opponent.[6] O'Neill, another

you the philanthropists of the religious world, or at least neutralize their opposition, and without their aid no *moral* victory can be achieved in this age and country." Letter to Sturge from Cobden, Nov. 21, 1841. *Memoirs*, p. 299.

[1] Richard, *Memoirs of Sturge*, p. 330.

[2] *Dictionary of National Biography*, vol. lviii, p. 358.

[3] Gammage, *op. cit.*, p. 32.

[4] *New History of Methodism*, vol. i, pp. 349, 399; *Methodist Minutes*, vol. ix, pp. 103, 111, 112.

[5] Gammage, *op. cit.*, p. 6.   [6] *Ibid.*, p. 7.

Chartist leader with an Irish name, ended his career as a Baptist minister, while neither O'Connor nor O'Brien could be reasonably accused of being Jesuits [1] by any one who had chanced to read the fiery denunciations of priestcraft which frequently appeared in their periodicals.[2]

The Catholics, like the Protestants, were not slow in making their influence felt in politics if their interests demanded it. The difference was that they wasted no time in pious protestations that it was no business of theirs as men of God.[3] Catholicism in Ireland had always been recognized as a leading influence in politics, and this influence Catholics did not hesitate to exert in England. Several Catholic priests attended and addressed the Anti-Corn Law Conference, and one, Rev. Thaddeus O'Malley, the famous Irish radical, became prominent in the latter stages of the Chartist movement, being elected delegate from Nottingham [4] to the National Assembly which met in London on May 1, 1848.

The poorest and most degraded part of the population of many of the English cities was composed largely of Irish immigrants, who were Catholics, of course, and often Chartists. But the participation of Catholicism in the Chartist movement was always casual and incidental, never in any way general or official.

With the adoption of more radical political views came the transition on the part of many Chartists to more radical religious views. Rev. Henry Solly and Rev. Joseph Barker, both leading Chartists, left the Presbyterian Church and the

---

[1] Stowell, *No Revolution.*

[2] *The Movement,* p. 303 (Aug. 24, 1844), reprints article from *Northern Star.* For O'Brien, see *The Social Reformer,* pp. 29, 84, and *McDouall's Chartist and Republican Journal,* pp. 149, 150.

[3] *Meth. Min.,* vol. viii, p. 105.

[4] Gammage, *op. cit.,* pp. 322, 324.

Methodist New Connexion, respectively, for Unitarianism. As with the ministers so with the workingmen. The wide range of thought allowed to Unitarians and the cultural emphasis in their teaching were very appealing to the Chartists and are excellently portrayed in *Alton Locke*.[1] A correspondent of *The People* writes of a village in Scotland (Tillicoultry) in which Unitarianism was the popular religion, due largely to the exertions of Mr. Browning, the Unitarian minister, who was a " Chartist, a Teetotaler, a Peace Advocate, and a true friend of Education ". W. J. Fox, noted Anti-Corn Law lecturer and political reformer, was perhaps the leading Unitarian minister in England.

The Tillicoultry correspondent, while admitting that not a few Unitarian Christians endeavor to make the profession of " their boasted recognition of the brotherhood of man " the standard for their political practice, yet fears that the habit is not so general as could be wished. He goes on to say that in the ten years he has been a Unitarian he has won more converts than many ministers and that he has succeeded best among the Chartists. This success he attributes chiefly to the fact that he endeavored " to make Christianity a practical thing ".[2]

Barker felt the opposition of the conservative Unitarians in an attack made upon him by the *Inquirer*, a Unitarian paper, in which he was characterized as " a destroyer of peace and order " and " an organ of discord and violence ", whose object was to stir up enmity among his fellow citizens and set the poor at war with the rich.[3] To this tirade Barker replied that the *Inquirer* no longer represented the

---

[1] Kingsley, *Alton Locke*, chap. xxii.
[2] *The People*, vol. i, p. 22.
[3] *Ibid.*, p. 22.

feelings of the majority of the Unitarians as it had under the editorship of William Hincks, but only of a small class of the less enlightened. To the group who were offended with his political proceedings and who believed that he was bringing dishonor upon the denomination,[1] he replied in a series of five articles [2] in which he sought to justify himself and vindicate Chartism in a discussion of each of its points. If the testimony of Barker is to be considered at all trustworthy it would seem that the Six Points found favor with a large class, if not a majority, of his denomination. In respect to this question as to many others of this discussion the sources are too meagre to allow of any definite statement.

IV. SCOTLAND

With the Scottish church torn by a religious strife which resulted in the secession of 1843 and the formation of the Free Church of Scotland there was little chance of the Chartist cause receiving much attention from either the wrought-up clergy who seceded or those who remained in the Establishment. The latter received, as in England, only abuse and condemnation from the Chartist press [3] and on the Chartist platform.[4]

The Established Church of Scotland did, however, boast of at least one political radical who stayed with it at the time of the secession. This was the famous Patrick Brewster (1788-1859) of Paisley. Noted among the free traders as the only member of the Established Church of Scotland who attended the Conference of Ministers at Manchester, he was equally beloved by the Chartists for his active and

[1] *The People*, vol. i, p. 4.

[2] *Ibid.*, pp. 4, 13, 28, 49, 57.

[3] *Chartist Circular*, p. 109.

[4] *Memoranda of the Chartist Agitation in Dundee*, pp. 34, 38; Gammage, *op. cit.*, p. 81.

unceasing coöperation. As early as the fall of 1838 he had assumed a leading position amongst the Moral Force Chartists of Scotland, and was on this point a strong antagonist of Feargus O'Connor, whom he thought an honest man but mistaken as to methods.[1] Brewster was a member of both the Complete Suffrage Convention and the Scottish Chartist Convention of 1842. As an advocate of teetotalism,[2] abolition of the slave trade, repeal of the Corn Laws, a national system of education, and the Charter, his whole life was a continual succession of disputes. The preaching of a series of sermons on Chartism and Militarism aroused the antagonism of the Paisley authorities. In conjunction with the Glasgow Presbytery they petitioned the Synod that he be removed on the charge of having preached a sermon in the Christian Chartist Church in Glasgow and thereby " giving countenance to a body of men, whose principles were unchristian and demoralizing ", conduct " highly censurable in any minister of the Gospel, involving a violation of the Ecclesiastical order, a contempt of decency, a profanation of the Lord's day, a desecration of the Christian ministry, and a mischievous encouragement of a system of disorganization and misrule both in Church and State." [3] The charge was dismissed but the Presbytery soon found opportunity for further complaint on the ground that Brewster had libelled the military. For this offense he was illegally suspended for a year, notwithstanding a memorial signed by 1,600 of his parishioners denying the charges and approving the discourses. The proceedings were eventually cancelled.[4] In the charges he had been accused of " per-

---

[1] Gammage, *op. cit.*, pp. 84, 198.
[2] *Chartist Circular*, pp. 284, 285.
[3] *The Seven Chartist and Military Discourses*, p. 410.
[4] *Ibid.*, p. 412.

version and prostitution of the ordinance of preaching"
by introducing into his discourses, "worldly and secular
politics and affairs", particularly "corn laws, poor laws
and the administration thereof, statements and sentiments
calculated to render those to whom they are addressed dis-
contented with their condition and to excite their passions".[1]
Always ready to do battle for the wrongs of the people,
Brewster carried his fight in behalf of the poor even into
the Assembly of the Church of Scotland.[2] His ministry in
Paisley covered about forty-one years.[3]

Although the Chartists naturally expected little sympathy
from the Established Church, they did on at least two occasions, endeavor to interest the secessionists, believing that
men with liberal ideas as to church government might be
affected similarly in regard to secular government. Added
force was given to this idea by the fact that Rev. John
Ritchie of Edinburgh, a universal suffragist, was a leader
in the secession movement. Consequently the Universal
Suffrage Central Committee of Scotland addressed a
memorial to the Relief Synod [4] and also to the United Secession Synod [5] urging upon the members in the name of all
that Christianity stood for to be "neither neutral nor in-
active in this great and holy warfare of principle".[6] It is
not recorded that these memorials made any impression or
met with any success.

[1] *The Seven Chartist and Military Discourses*, p. 416.

[2] *Ibid.*, p. 421.

[3] *Dictionary of National Biography*, vol. vi, p. 304.

[4] *Chartist Circular*, p. 141.

[5] *Ibid.*, p. 161.

[6] *Ibid.*, p. 141.

CHAPTER IV

Positive Contribution of the Church to the Chartist Movement

I. THE WORK OF THE CLERGY

HAVING attempted to diagnose the attitude of the average English workingman towards Christianity as exemplified in the British churches and having examined the general feeling on the part of the churches towards the Chartist movement, it remains in the final chapter only to gather the threads together and to put into concrete form the actual contributions of the church to the agitation for the People's Charter and "the first workingmen's party of modern times ".[1] Although " both chapel and church were largely hostile to the Chartist movement ",[2] there was, as we have seen, on the part of not a few individuals officially connected with organized Christianity a sympathy for a more complete democracy and a willingness to work and suffer in the cause.

The most obvious way to be of service was to aid in public meetings and, especially in the early years of the movement, it was not an infrequent spectacle to behold ministers of various denominations gracing the stage at the huge open-air gatherings and torch-light processions. Rev. Arthur S. Wade of London, clergyman of the Established Church and one of the deputies of the London Workingmen's Association appointed to attend a Glasgow demon-

[1] Engels, *Socialism Utopian and Scientific*, Intro., p. xxx.
[2] Hall, *op. cit.*, p. 173.

stration,[1] addressed a meeting estimated at 200,000,[2] and
in September of the same year was one of the speakers at
the Palace Yard meeting in Birmingham.[3] Patrick Brewster
of the Scotch Establishment did not confine his Chartist
discourses to his pulpit but was a frequent speaker at Chartist gatherings, thereby incurring the wrath of O'Connor,
whose Physical Force ravings he strenuously opposed, especially in a speech at Carlton Hill, Edinburgh.[4] Rev. W.
J. Fox, Unitarian, was a speaker with Wade at the Palace
Yard meeting, while Rev. J. C. Meeke, Unitarian, and Rev.
John Jenkinson of Kettering addressed the Chartists of
Northampton in 1838 from the same platform.[5] Rev.
William Hill, Swedenborgian and O'Connor's right-hand
man, was a prominent orator during the entire period.
Joseph Barker came forward as a Chartist lecturer during
the revival of 1848.[6] J. R. Stephens, however, was un-
doubtedly the most noted minister in any way connected
with the movement.[7] Many others were occasional speakers.

The prominence of these ministers in the cause of reform
led the Chartists in several instances to elect them to official
standing in the movement. To the first and most famous
convention which met in London in February, 1839, one
clergyman of the Church of England and one Dissenting
minister were elected.[8] Dr. Wade represented Nottingham[9]
and took a leading part in the convention until he with many

[1] Gammage, *op. cit.*, p. 21.
[2] *Ibid.*, p. 20.
[3] *Ibid.*, p. 47.
[4] *Ibid.*, p. 84.
[5] *Ibid.*, p. 37.
[6] *Ibid.*, p. 323.
[7] *Ibid.*, pp. 56 *et seq.*
[8] Lovett, *op. cit.*, p. 201.
[9] Gammage, *op. cit.*, p. 68.

others, resigned when the Physical Force party became dominant.[1] Stephens was elected for Ashley [2] but later resigned,[3] although he seems to have been present at the convention.[4] To the National Assembly which met on May 1, 1848, Joseph Barker and Thaddeus O'Malley, the latter a Catholic priest and political radical, were elected to represent Leeds and Nottingham respectively.[5] At the London Convention of 1851, Rev. A. Duncanson, Congregationalist, represented the Paisley district. Patrick Brewster represented Paisley in the Scottish Convention of 1842. On the Birmingham provisional committee for the Complete Suffrage Conference of 1842 was the Rev. James Alsop, while the following ministers were listed as attending: J. Jenkinson, of Kettering; Noah Jones, Derby; Charles Kirkland, Newark; Edward Miall, Stoke Newington; T. Harwood Morgan, Stourbridge; J. P. Mursell, Leicester; John Ritchie, Edinburgh; Henry Solly, Yeovil and Bridport; Thomas Spencer, Bath; William Thomas, Fairfield, and Arthur S. Wade, London.[6]

Not only were ministers occasional representatives to Chartist conventions but in several instances the conventions were held in churches. The Scotch Chartist Convention which met August 15, 1841, at Glasgow, met in the Universalist Church,[7] and the Scotch convention of 1842 was also held in a church.[8] The conference of operatives held in Manchester on August 12th, which preceded the

[1] Gammage, *op. cit.*, p. 156.
[2] *Ibid.*, p. 62.   [3] *Ibid.*, p. 67.
[4] Lovett, *op. cit.*, p. 207; Holyoake, *Life of Stephens*, p. 143.
[5] Gammage, *op. cit.*, pp. 322, 324.
[6] *Minutes of the Conference*, p. 41. See below for discussion of Complete Suffrage Conference, p. 110.
[7] *Chartist Circular*, preface, p. iv.
[8] *Ibid.*, p. 511.

Lancashire riots of 1842, seems to have been held at the chapel of Scholefield.[1]

In the field of journalism some notable work was accomplished in the cause of democracy by ministers. William Hill, until his quarrel with O'Connor, edited the *Northern Star*, the most popular of the Chartist periodicals. Edward Miall permitted the *Nonconformist* to be used as the official organ of the Complete Suffrage Union and brilliantly upheld in its columns the principles of universal suffrage. Joseph Barker was the publisher of *The People,* a weekly periodical with a circulation of 20,000, and *The Reformer's Almanac.* J. R. Stephens edited *The Champion,* a radical paper for workingmen, although hardly an advocate of Chartism.

Not only as editors did many of the ministers assist the Chartists but as pamphleteers as well. Some of the editorials of Miall were reprinted as pamphlets and issued by the National Complete Suffrage Union.[2] This association published other tracts from the pens of clergymen, among which were *The Suffrage Demonstrated to be the Right of All Men, by an Appeal to Scripture and Common Sense,* being the substance of a lecture delivered March, 1843, by Rev. J. E. Giles of Leeds, and *The People's Rights, and How to Get Them,* by Rev. Thomas Spencer, M. A.[3]

---

[1] Gammage, *op. cit.*, pp. 218, 235.

[2] See also *National Reform Tracts,* nos. 18, 19, 20.

[3] See *Dictionary of National Biography, loc. cit.*, for a list. The following is the list of what Spencer considers the people's rights: "(1) The right to earn a living with the fewest possible impediments. (2) The right to keep property when acquired with the fewest possible demands upon it. (3) The right of every man to worship God according to his conscience. (4) The right of good government. (5) The right to self-government by full, fair, and free representation." Under this head he recognizes the necessity of practically all of the demands of the Charter— *The People's Rights, and How to Get Them.*

Spencer wrote a long series of pamphlets of an extremely radical type, on political and church reform, which aroused the *Christian Remembrancer* to demand how it happened that a clergyman " should be allowed to propagate such pestilential opinions . . . without being made to feel the just punishment for his apostasy by being degraded and excommunicated ".[1]   Benjamin Parsons, Congregationalist, also wrote a series of pamphlets on reform called *Tracts for the Fustian Jackets and Smock Frocks.*[2]   Rev. Henry Solly wrote at some length on *What Says Christianity to the Present Distress?*, while Rev. Alexander Duncanson wrote a tract on *The Political Rights of the People.*   Brewster's political sermons were published in book form under the title of *The Seven Chartist and Military Discourses Libelled by the Marquis of Abercam, and Other Heritors of the Abby Parish.*   Most of these tracts written by ministers are an attempt to reconcile democracy with Christianity and to prove that support of universal suffrage is demanded from a professor of Christianity.

At least two ministers were imprisoned for their activities in the Chartist movement.   J. R. Stephens on August 10, 1839, was convicted of using seditious language at Hyde and sentenced to eighteen months imprisonment and the giving of sureties for five years.[3]   W. V. Jackson was convicted of seditious conspiracy on March 24, 1840 at Liverpool assizes and sentenced to two years imprisonment and the finding of sureties for three years.[4]   Several others were

---

[1] *Christian Remembrancer*, vol. v, p. 441.

[2] Hood, *The Earnest Minister* (London, 1846), pp. 271 *et seq.;* also appendix of his *Life*, p. 500.

[3] *Parliamentary Accounts and Papers*, 1840, vol. xxxviii, no. 600, p. 4; Gammage, *op. cit.*, p. 157.

[4] *Parliamentary Accounts and Papers*, 1840, vol. xxxviii, no. 600, p. 8; Gammage, *op. cit.*, pp. 178, 179.

arrested and hailed into court but finally discharged, among whom were William Essler, dissenting minister, for conspiracy,[1] William Davies, dissenting minister, for harboring his nephew, a traitor,[2] and James Scholefield, with fifty-eight others, because he

did unlawfully aid, abet, assist, comfort, support, and encourage certain evil-disposed persons to continue and persist in unlawful assemblies, threats, intimidation, and violence; and in impeding and stopping of the labour employed in certain trades, manufactories, and business with intent thereby to cause terror and alarm in the minds of the peaceable subjects of this realm, and by the means of such terror and alarm, violently and unlawfully to cause and procure certain great changes in the constitution of this realm, as by law established.[3]

Joseph Barker was arrested in 1848 on the charge of conspiracy and sedition but was offered his discharge on condition of entering into his own recognizance to appear when called upon. Having fifty witnesses ready he refused and demanded a trial. " The Attorney General fumed and fretted, and the judge insulted; but at last they gave up the task ", and the former entered a *nolle prosequi.*[4]

II. THE COMPLETE SUFFRAGE MOVEMENT

The Complete Suffrage movement has already been mentioned several times. It was the single part of the struggle for democracy during the last hundred years in England in which the influence of the clergy and ministers was important, if not dominant. The Complete Suffrage movement, in the words of its founders, was simply an attempt

[1] *Parliamentary Accounts and Papers*, 1840, vol. xxxviii, no. 600, p. 6.
[2] *Ibid.*, p. 6.
[3] Gammage, *op. cit.*, pp. 232, 235.
[4] *Ibid.*, p. 343; Barker, *Modern Skepticism: A Life Story*, p. 252.

"to unite two dissevered classes, on the question of parliamentary reform", and "by peaceful and Christian means alone" effect "a full, fair, and free representation of the people in the British House of Commons".[1] It was distinguished from Chartism in its demands in that it insisted primarily upon only one of the Six Points; universal manhood suffrage. In its antecedents it emanated distinctly from the middle class, and included the members of the bourgeoisie who believed that the Reform Bill of 1832 fell short of a just and ideal representation.

Many middle-class clergy and laymen had long deplored the distrust evinced toward them by the working classes and the consequent alienation of those classes from all institutions looked upon as characteristically bourgeois, in particular the church. It was this situation that led Edward Miall in the *Nonconformist* to urge upon his middle-class constituency the justice of the new demands, and their duty as Christians of healing the breach between the two classes by actively aiding in the fight for universal suffrage. The *Eclectic Review*, another church magazine which coöperated with Miall, bluntly reduced the matter to an affair of political expediency when it said: "To expect to make head against a Tory government with divided forces is chimerical; and to work for a coöperation of the industrious classes without an equitable regard to their claims is to insure to ourselves defeat and ruin."[2]

The work begun by Miall in his notable articles was taken up by Joseph Sturge upon his return from America, when he assumed the leadership as the one man in England best calculated to conciliate all classes. The campaign to bring all classes together on the basis of a reform of the franchise

[1] *Minutes of the Proceedings of the Conference*, p. 3.
[2] April, 1843.

was begun at a conference of Anti-Corn Law deputies on Wednesday, November 17, 1841, at the conclusion of which Sturge, in an especially convened meeting, brought forward his project. It was determined that a declaration should be drawn up and distributed and a conference held of its supporters. The idea was enthusiastically approved and the conference convened on April 5th at Birmingham, composed of middle-class reformers and Moral Force Chartists to the number of eighty-seven from England and four from Ireland, including seventeen ministers. On the executive committee were Rev. Noah Jones, Rev. Thomas Spencer, Rev. Henry Solly and Rev. Edward Miall. The platform of this conference was set forth in a Bill of Rights which, in order to hold the Chartists, included each of the Six Points, later embraced in a petition to the House of Commons.[1] Much emphasis was laid in the conference upon the conception of Christian duty in its relation to the suffrage and the conciliatory spirit shown on both sides insured the meeting's success. Addresses were issued to both the middle and working classes. Sharman Crawford, a few days later (April 21, 1842) on behalf of the conference tested the complete suffrage strength in the House. For the motion to consider the proposition he secured seventy-four votes.

The conference of April, however, was only preliminary to a bigger convention which met in December of the same year. To this convention the enfranchised and unenfranchised were allowed an equal number of delegates, but the bickerings over representation augured ill for the success of the impending assembly. The spirit of the April gathering was lacking in December and a break came on the very first motion made, that to make the Bill of Rights, accepted

[1] *Vide* appendix i.

in April, the basis of the discussion of the conference.
To many Chartists the Bill of Rights was unknown, while
many others who had worked and suffered for the Charter
were unwilling to give up even the name. Lovett, to the
surprise of many, opposed the motion and moved for a
consideration of the Charter. A long discussion followed
in which Miall, Brewster and Spencer spoke for the Bill
of Rights and Wade for the Charter. The Complete Suffrage party refused a compromise and neither side would
back down. A vote being taken, which resulted in a
victory for the Charter, Sturge announced that he and his
followers felt bound to retire and sit in a separate body.
The Chartists after a period of confusion and strife broke
up. The Complete Suffrage party likewise failed to make
much headway and the failure of the two classes to come
to a mutual understanding at this conference put any hope
of a near success of the Charter out of the question. The
Sturgeites laid the blame of the result upon the Chartists,
maintaining that they had sacrificed the reality of a great
political gain for the sentiment of a name.[1] The Chartists
accused the middle class of lack of sympathy and of attempting by a strategical political move to hold them at
arm's-length.[2]

The Complete Suffrage movement, says Sturge's biographer, " breathed for the first time since the return of the
Stuarts, a Christian principle into political action ".[3] There
is a large element of truth in this statement, but the plea for
a close connection between Christianity and politics which
was made so much of during the convening of the confer-

[1] Solly, *These Eighty Years*, vol. i, p. 408.
[2] Cooper, *Life of Thomas Cooper*, p. 222.
[3] Richard, Henry, *Memoirs of Joseph Sturge*, p. 329.

ences, the launching of the new movement,[1] and the April gathering, was sadly lacking in the Birmingham conference of December. A trifle more of it might have turned the scale [2] and given a different history to what resulted in dismal failure.[3]

In the study of the relationship between the Chartist movement and the church two facts stand forth preëminently. In the first place, none of the denominations seemed to be able to break away from the prejudices and viewpoint of the class which it represented, or to put itself in the attitude of the Chartists who thought that Christianity was vitally concerned in giving them what they considered their just rights and a chance to help themselves. The churches which did not go on record as absolutely opposed to Chartism looked upon it coldly and with suspicion. What coöperation or sympathy the movement received was mainly from the small group of ministers whose activities have just been recounted, who either believed in democracy for its own sake or else had become convinced, with the Chartists, that it was the duty of all Christians to aid in the political emancipation of their fellow-men.

The second point is no less significant than the first. Although these pages are not intended as a vindication of Chartism or any other democratic movement, it is interesting to note that the " lawless " and " dangerous " democrats were the leaders in their day in the movement not only for a reform in the government, but also for one in the church, for universal and secular education, for teetotalism, pacifism, the abolition of the death penalty,

[1] *Supra*, pp. 22, 23.

[2] Cooper, *op. cit.*, p. 222.

[3] On the Complete Suffrage Movement, see Gammage, *op. cit.*, pp. 241 *et seq.;* Cooper's *Life*, pp. 221 *et seq.;* Solly, *These Eighty Years*, vol. i, pp. 376-384, 404-408, and the *Eclectic Review* for April, 1843.

direct taxation and many other principles which to-day
are either accepted without question or are still goals
of endeavors.   Even the Charter itself has largely been
incorporated into the law of England. Organized Christianity deliberately refused the leadership in political and
social reformation, and the burden was taken up by the
proletariat. The necessity thrown upon the workingmen
of leading the fight for reform in all departments gave to
Chartism an intellectual and ethical stimulus which made it
probably the most important social movement in nineteenth-
century England.

APPENDIX I

PETITION OF THE COMPLETE SUFFRAGE CONFERENCE OF APRIL, 1842, TO THE HOUSE OF COMMONS

Sheweth,

That in the opinion of your petitioners, every member of society has an equal right with every other member to have a voice in making the laws which he is called upon to obey.

That this just principle has already been recognized in the British Constitution, for by various ancient statutes it is provided, " that no person be compelled to pay any tax or make any loan to the king against his will," and by a statute of King Edward III, it is declared, that " such laws are against reason and the franchise of the land," which enactments are confirmed and expounded by the celebrated petition of right, which provides that " no man be compelled to make or yield any gift or tax, without common consent, by act of parliament."

That the principle is further sanctioned by the dictates of that holy religion, which teaches men to do to others, as they would that others should do unto them.

That in carrying out this principle, only such limitations or restrictions should be allowed as naturally arise out of the right itself, as are necessary to its practical exercise,—and as are equally applicable to all classes of the community.

That, therefore your petitioners, after due deliberation, have arrived at the conviction, that the elective franchise ought to be extended to every man of twenty-one years of age, who is not deprived of his rights of citizenship, in consequence of the verdict of a jury of his countrymen.

That a false principle of representation namely, that of property and not persons—having been acted on for a great length of time in this country, many abuses have thereby arisen and been perpetuated; and that as the removal of these abuses is necessary in order to render complete suffrage, as defined in the preceding propositions, practically beneficial, your petitioners are of the opinion that the details embodied in the following propositions are essential for rendering the representation of the people on the fundamental principle already declared, full, fair, and free.

That every man ought to be able and willing to give an open and conscientious vote—yet under the present circumstances of the country, and with the general prevalence of bribery and intimidation, that the system of voting by ballot should be adopted, in order effectually to secure the free exercise of the suffrage, which free exercise is sanctioned by acts of parliament declaring that " elections ought to be free."

That for the purpose of securing a fair and equal representation of the people, it is necessary that the whole country be divided into districts each containing, as nearly as may be, an equal number of electors.

That all legal election expenses, and a reasonable remuneration to Members of Parliament for their services, ought to be borne at the public expense.

That it is of great importance to secure and maintain the responsibility of members to their constituents, and your petitioners are of the opinion that annual parliaments are a proper means for securing this object.

May it therefore please the Commons to resolve itself into a committee of the whole house, to take these premises into its deliberate consideration, or adopt such other measures as shall secure a full, fair, and free representation of the people, according to the fundamental principles hereinbefore stated.

Your petitioners, in conclusion, would express their heartfelt prayer, that Almighty God may direct your councils, for the happiness of the nation, the welfare of mankind in general, and for His own glory.

From the *Minutes of the Proceedings at the Conference of Representatives of the Middle and Working Classes of Great Britain, Held First at the Waterloo Rooms, and Afterwards at the Town Hall, Birmingham,* pp. 19, 20, 21.

APPENDIX II

Chartist Gospel—A New Revelation

THE BOOK OF THE CHRONICLES OF THE DEMOCRATS

Chapter I

1. Victoria being Queen of the Isles and of extensive countries abroad, Sir Robert Peel being Prime Minister, Sir James Graham being Secretary for the Home Department, and the Earl de Grey being Governor of the Land of Erin.

2. In those days came Feargus O'Connor, preaching to the whole people of the United Queendom of Great Britain and Ireland.

3. Saying, the day of justice draweth nigh, for the masses are awakening from their sleep.

4. But when he saw the Tories, and the Whigs, and the Corn-Law Repealers, come to hear, he said unto them, O generation of vipers, what hath induced you to fleece and rob the people.

5. And think not to say unto yourselves we are just before God; Amen, I say unto you, Repent lest you may be punished for your evil deeds.

6. For reason is gone abroad and will soon penetrate the minds of all men, and will force them to become lovers of liberty.

7. And thus did Feargus O'Connor harass the tyrants, and despots and oppressors of every kind, even from the days of William the Foolish and the sixth year of the reign of Victoria.

8. And the lawyers, and chief priests, and factory masters conspired together to put him to death, but they could not for fear of the people.

587]   123

9. But they put him into prison for the long space of sixteen months; even in York castle did they confine him:

10. So that his fame extended to all parts of the world where democracy is known; from the banks of the Thames to the banks of the sire of rivers.

11. In the sixth year of the reign of Victoria, the first and last, he went to the city of long chimneys and cotton factories to instruct the people, and thousands of thousands of people came from the surrounding towns to hear him.

12. And he opened his mouth and taught them saying;

13. Ye Chartists are the salt of the earth: Ye are the light of the world: let your light so shine before men that they may see the truths of the Charter, and seeing believe.

14. Think not I am come to destroy the Constitution; no, but to restore it: nor to injure life; no, but to preserve it. I am come to assist the needy, to instruct the ignorant, to confirm the timid, to raise you from slavery, and to establish justice.

15. No man can serve two masters; for either he will hate the one and love the other, or he will hold to the one and despise the other. Ye cannot serve Whiggism and Toryism with Chartism.

16. Judge not rashly or unjustly, lest that you yourselves might be so judged; for most assuredly will the people hold those that dispense justice responsible for their acts.

17. Beware of false teachers and pretended friends who come to you in sheep's clothing, but who inwardly are ravenous wolves.

18. Therefore, whosoever heareth these sayings of mine, and doeth them, I will liken him unto a wise man who built his home upon a rock and the storms arose and prevailed not against it.

19. And it came to pass as Feargus O'Connor sojourned to an inn for refreshment, he saw Jonathan Bairstow; and he said unto him, Follow thou me. And when he sat down to eat with working men, and when the Whigs and Tories saw it, they marvelled amongst themselves that he should do this.

20. And the names of a few of the great apostles of Chartism were F. O'Connor, the son of Roger and nephew of Arthur, and James Leach, and Peter Murray McDouall, and John Campbell and J. A. R. Bairstow, and R. K. Philp, and William Hill and James Scholefield, and Morgan Williams, and George Julian Harney, and George White, and Thomas Cooper, and Christopher Doyle, and Bernard McCartney, and Thomas Clarke, and James McArthur, and John Duncan, and Robert Lowrie, and William Beesley, and Ruffy Ridley, and Thomas Wheeler. And there were hundreds of disciples of this great party in all parts of the Western Isles.

The Penny Democrat and Political Illuminator, pp. 17, 18 (no date).

APPENDIX III

That the Church of England and Chartism totally oppose each other, produce wholly different effects, and lead to widely and utterly different destinations, will appear if we just consider to what they each lead.

Chartism	*The Church of England*
Leads to unholy desires, wicked counsels and unjust works.	Leads us to pray to that God from whom "All holy desires, all good counsel and all just works proceed."
—to perils, dangers, evil and mischief.	—" us to pray to be kept from all perils and dangers, from all evil and mischief."
—" to battle, murder and sudden death."	—us to pray and be delivered " from battle, and murder and sudden death."
—us to curse and oppose the magistrates in the execution of their duties, in punishing wickedness and vice.	—us to beseech God, " to bless and keep the magistrates, giving them grace to execute justice and maintain truth."
—all nations to war, hatred and discord.	—us to ask God " to give to all nations, unity, peace, and concord."
—men out of the way of truth, into error and deception.	—us to pray that God " may bring into the way of truth, all such as have erred and are deceived."

126

[590

Chartism

—to danger, necessity, and tribulation; and leaves those that are led by it helpless and comfortless.

—to the murder of fathers and husbands; and leaves the fatherless children and widows desolate and oppressed.

—to the disturbance of public worship, to the immediate dispersion of the congregation when in the middle of their devotions, at the sight of the pike, pistol, scythe, gun, etc.

—to scepticism, infidelity, and disbelief of the Scriptures.

—to evils which we, on account of our sins have righteously deserved.

The Church of England

—us to beseech God that He "may be pleased to recover, help, and comfort, all that are in danger, necessity and tribulation."

—us to ask God "that it may please Him to defend and provide for the fatherless children and widows, and all that are desolate and oppressed."

—us to pray thus, "Grant O Lord we beseech Thee, that the course of this world may be so peaceably ordered by thy governance, that thy Church may joyfully serve thee in all godly quietness."

—us to pray God "to grant us grace to hear, read, mark, learn, and inwardly digest them."

—us to beseech God "graciously to hear us, that those evils, which the craft and subtilty of the devil or man worketh against us, be brought to naught."

Chartism	*The Church of England*
—professors of religion to bring reproach upon the Gospel, by their wicked and evil deeds.	—us to ask Almighty God, to " grant unto all them that are admitted into the fellowship of Christ's religion, that they may eschew those things that are contrary to their profession and follow all such things as are agreeable to the same."
—to anarchy; to disobey and rebel against the powers that be; and to the subversion of all good government.	—us and all subjects duly to consider whose authority the Queen hath, that we may " faithfully serve, honor, and humbly obey her."
—to poverty, misery, and transportation; the gallows, death and hell.	—to wealth, peace, freedom, pardon; and beseeches the Lord in his boundless mercy and love to " deliver us from wrath and from everlasting damnation."

Jenkin's *Chartism Unmasked*, 19th ed., pp. 25-27 (Merthyr Tydvil, 1840).

APPENDIX IV

A Prayer

RECENTLY DELIVERED AT THE OPENING OF A CHARTIST CHURCH
IN LONDON

O Lord, the fountain of all goodness, by whom our valleys at this time are covered with corn, and our hills teeming with innumerable flocks, the Maker of one blood of all nations that dwell upon the face of the earth, and who hath declared Thyself no respecter of persons by levelling crowned heads with beggars in one mighty sepulchre, and mingling the dust of proud and haughty tyrants with that of the meanest slave. Ere our lips give utterance, thou art acquainted with our desires and the interests of our hearts, the cruel and wicked judgments of which the tribunals of the land resound, are all naked before Thee, and no secret can be hid. Hear the prayer of Thy persecuted servant, and the silent breathings of the oppressed that surround him, on behalf of those of our brethren by whom Thy violated law hath spoken out and for which they are now breathing the polluted air of the dungeon, reduced to skeletons, with the months of their harsh and rigorous endurance. Be Thou with them, support them, preserve them, and teach them, that they may come forth from the prison cell, as giants refreshed with new wine, mighty in power to the pulling down of the strongholds of corruption, and in boldness and self possession work out the political redemption of the British People. O Lord, hasten the long wished for period, when such men as honest O'Connor, Vincent, Lovett, Collins, and many others, shall shake the Senate House by their eloquence, and direct the realm by their wisdom, that iniquity may be compelled to hide her head, and the iron rod of despotism be for ever broken; when the laws for the separation of husband and wife shall be no more; when those ties that have been so rudely broken, shall again be united; when bastiles, the monuments of wicked legislation, shall tumble to the ground, and peace be proclaimed upon earth, and good will amongst men. Hear us, O Lord, on behalf of a wicked and persecuting church, which exists by violence and plundering of goods, instead of the freewill offerings of the heart; convert our bishops and clergy to Christianity, and release the martyr Thorogood from gaol. May tithe-barns cease to be their temples and money their God. May they abandon all choice schemes which tend to the destruction of liberty and genuine knowledge. While thus assembled to offer prayers to Thee, we supplicate for her who sits upon a human bone-and-blood built throne, swaying the sceptre of this mighty empire; may she henceforth counsel her wicked councilors, and teach her foolish senators wisdom; that her people's requests may be granted, and herself in reality be Queen Victoria by the grace of God, instead of queen of slaves. Hear us on behalf of the countless thousands of India, whom designing men are seeking to destroy by the game of horror and war; may we, as a nation and a people, refuse to take part in the shedding of human blood, and show the world, by our lives and conduct, we are determined to obey God rather than man. We pray for all sorts and conditions of men, for all spies, for all false witnesses, for all perjured jurors, for all unjust judges, and for all the victims made now at home and abroad; aid and assist us in the mighty work we have to perform; prepare us to brave persecution, and enable us to surmount every difficulty and may we never relax our exertions until our birthright, the Charter, do come. That on earth, as in heaven, Thy will may be done. To this may all our hearts respond, and every tongue exclaim Amen.

The Chartist Circular, p. 211 (Sept. 19, 1840).

APPENDIX V

RULES AND OBJECTS OF THE EAST LONDON CHARTIST TEMPERANCE ASSOCIATION

(Recommended by the *English Chartist Circular*, p. 19, vol. i, to its constituents for the formation of similar associations.)

1. That this association be denominated the Chartist Temperance Association.

2. That the affairs of this Association shall be managed by a Committee of ten, chosen from the first members who join it.

3. That the Members and Committee shall be elected every three months. Seven to be a quorum.

4. That the Committee shall meet once a week; or oftener, if necessary.

5. That there be a general meeting of the Association once every month for the admission of Members—to receive reports and for the transaction of general business.

6. That no rule or article shall be altered without the consent of a majority of the Members, all of whom shall receive a week's notice of the same.

7. That each Member be recommended to subscribe One Penny per week to defray the expenses of the Association.

8. That it be the duty of this Association to advance the moral and intellectual welfare of the Members; by lectures, discussions, or any other means.

9. That the members of the Association are earnestly recommended to take an interest in the welfare of each other by trading with, and endeavoring to procure employment for, any of the Members who are in want of the same; and in order to facilitate this object a record of each member's trade or occupation be kept by the Secretary, and read over at the general monthly meetings of the Association.

10. That as early as the Funds will allow, a convenient place shall be hired for the use of the Association: and a library of useful books be established in order that the Members may spend their leisure hours profitably, and set a good example.

11. That the Members of this Association adopt as their motto the following beautiful rule of justice — "Do unto others as ye would they should do unto you."

12. In order that harmony of sentiment and unanimity of action may characterize the Association, all discussion on questions of Theology is expressly forbidden.

13. That persons desirous of becoming Members of this Association must abstain from all intoxicating drinks for one week previous to their admission, in order to try the principle and prevent a relapse.

14. That to prevent embarrassment in the pecuniary affairs of the Association, the Committee will not allow the debts of the Association to exceed at any time the sum of ten shillings, except by the consent of the majority of the Members, given at any public meeting.

15. That the following be the pledge and qualification of membership.

I voluntarily consent to abstain from all intoxicating liquors, except prescribed by a medical person; and, as temperance applies to all things, I renounce the use of tobacco as a common habit, injurious alike to health and good morals, and pledge myself not to use it, except as a medicine; and do further declare that I will use all moral and lawful means to cause the People's Charter to become the law of the land.

APPENDIX VI

CHARLES KINGSLEY'S APPEAL TO THE CHARTISTS, APRIL 12, 1848

WORKMEN OF ENGLAND

You say that you are wronged. Many of you are wronged; and many besides yourselves know it. Almost all men who have heads and hearts know it—above all, the working clergy know it. They go into your houses, they see the shameful filth and darkness in which you are forced to live crowded together; they see your children growing up in ignorance and temptation, for want of fit education; they see intelligent and well-read men among you, shut out from a Freeman's just right of voting; and they see too the noble patience and self-control with which you have as yet borne these evils. They see it, and God sees it.

Workmen of England! You have more friends than you think for. Friends who expect nothing from you, but who love you, because you are their brothers, and who fear God, and therefore dare not neglect you, His children; men who are drudging and sacrificing themselves to get you your rights; men who know what your rights are, better than you know yourselves, who are trying to get for you something nobler than charters and dozens of Acts of Parliament—more useful than this " fifty thousandth share in a Talker in the National Palaver at Westminster " can give you. You may disbelieve them, insult them—you cannot stop their working for you, beseeching you as you love yourselves, to turn back from the precipice of riot, which ends in the gulf of universal distrust, stagnation, starvation.

You think the Charter would make you free—would to

597]   133

God it would! The Charter is not bad; *if the men who use it are not bad!* But will the Charter make you free? Will it free you from slavery to ten-pound bribes? Slavery to beer and gin? Slavery to every spouter who flatters your self-conceit, and stirs up bitterness and headlong rage in you? That, I guess, is real slavery; to be a slave to one's own stomach, one's own pocket, one's own temper. Will the Charter cure that? Friends, you want more than Acts of Parliament can give.

Englishmen! Saxons! Workers of the great, cool-headed, strong-handed nation of England, the workshop of the world, the leader of freedom for seven hundred years, men say you have common sense! then do not humbug yourselves into meaning "license," when you cry for "liberty"; who would dare refuse you freedom? for the Almighty God, and Jesus Christ, the poor Man, who died for poor men, will bring it about for you, though all the Mammonites of the earth were against you. A nobler day is dawning for England, a day of freedom, science, industry!

But there will be no true freedom without virtue, no true science without religion, no true industry without the fear of God, and love to your fellow-citizens.

Workers of England, be wise, and then you *must* be free, for you will be *fit* to be free.

A Working Parson.

Charles Kingsley, *His Letters and Memories of His Life*, edited by his wife, 10th ed. (London, 1878), vol. i, pp. 156-157.

BIBLIOGRAPHY

LIBRARIES

Most of the periodicals and pamphlets listed below were consulted in the private library of Professor E. R. A. Seligman. There are, however, quite a few Chartist pamphlets on the shelves of the New York Public Library, while several of the important periodicals are to be found in the Columbia Library. The Yale Library also contains a few of the sources. The library of the Drew Theological Seminary is particularly rich in Methodist literature, containing, as it does, the Osborn and Tyerman collections of early pamphlets. The Union Theological Seminary library contains a collection of the works of Joseph Barker, as well as a large number of nineteenth century Catholic pamphlets.

REFERENCE WORKS

Parliamentary Accounts and Pap. rs.
Encyclopædia Britannica, Ninth Edition, 1887. Article on Methodism. Also Eleventh Edition (N. Y., 1911).
New International Encyclopædia, Second Edition, 1914-1916.
Dictionary of National Biography. Edited by Leslie Stephens, 1885-1912.

CONTEMPORARY CONDITIONS IN ENGLAND

Engels, Frederick, *The Condition of the Working Class in England in 1844* (London, ed. 1892).
———, *Socialism, Utopian and Scientific.* Translated by E. Aveling (London, 1892).
Gibbins, H. de B., *Industry in England*, 7th ed (New York, 1912).
Knight, Charles, *A Popular History of England* (London, 1863-1868).
Lecky, W. E. H., *History of England in the Eighteenth Century*, 8 vols. (1878-1890).
McCarthy, Justin, *A History of Our Own Times from the Accession of Queen Victoria to the General Election of 1880*, 4 vols (London, 1880). Three additional vols. bring this down to 1901 (London, 1897-1905).
Marriott, J. A. R., *England Since Waterloo* (N. Y. and London, 1913).
Martineau, Harriet, *A History of the Thirty Years' Peace, 1816-1846* (London, 1877).

Molesworth, William, *The History of England* (London, 1874).
Political History of England, ed. by Wm. Hunt and R. L. Poole in twelve volumes. Vol. 12, by S. Low and L. C. Sanders, covers the period from 1837-1901.
Prentice, Archibald, *History of the Anti-Corn Law League,* 2 vols. (London, 1853).
Rose, J. Holland, *The Rise and Growth of Democracy in Great Britain* (London, 1897).
Rogers, J. E. T., *Six Centuries of Work and Wages,* 6th ed. (London, 1901).
Seligman, E. R. A., "Owen and the Christian Socialists," *Political Science Quarterly,* vol. i, pp. 208-249.
Slater, Gilbert, *The Making of Modern England.* Revised edition (Boston and New York, 1915).
Traill, H. D., and J. S. Mann, *Social England.* Illustrated edition, 6 vols. in 12 (London, 1909).
Walpole, Spencer, *A History of England from the Conclusion of the Great War,* 6 vols. (London, rev. ed., 1902-5).
Weber, A. F., *Growth of Cities in the Nineteenth Century* (N. Y., 1899).

CHARTISM

1. *General Works*

Brewster, Patrick, *The Seven Chartist and Military Discourses Libeled by the Marquis of Abercam, and the Other Heritors of the Abbey Parish* (Paisley, 1843).
Carlyle, Thomas, *Chartism* (1839).
Dierlamm, Gotthilf, *Die Flugschriftenliteratur der Chartistenbewegung und ihr Widerhall in der öffentlichen Meinung* (Leipzig, 1909).
Dolleans, Edouard, *Le Chartisme,* 2 vols. (Paris, 1912).
Gammage, R. G., *History of the Chartist Movement, 1837-1854* (London, new ed., 1894).
Jones, E. D., *Chartism—A Chapter in English Industrial History. Transactions of the Wisconsin Society of Sciences, Arts and Letters,* vol. xii, part ii (Madison, 1900).
Schlüter, Hermann, *Die Chartisten-bewegung; ein Beitrag zu sozial-politischen Geschichte Englands* (N. Y., 1916).
Tildsley, John L., *Die Entstehung und die ökonomischen Grundsätze der Chartistenbewegung* (Jena, 1898).

2. *Novels*

Disraeli, Benjamin, *Coningsby, or The New Generation* (London, 1844, new edition, 1871).
———, *Sybil, or The Two Nations* (London, 1845, new edition, 1871).
Gaskell, Elizabeth G., *Mary Barton* (1848).

Kingsley, Charles, *Alton Locke* (New York edition, 1850).
——, *Yeast* (London, 1851).
Solly, Henry, *James Woodford, Carpenter and Chartist*, 2 vols. (London, 1881).

3. *Biographies*

Bamford, Samuel, *Passages in the Life of a Radical*, 2 vols. (London, 1844).
Barker, J. T., *The Life of Joseph Barker* (London, 1880).
Barker, Joseph, *Modern Skepticism: A Journey Through the Land of Doubt and Back Again. A Life Story.* (Philadelphia, 1874.)
——, *Teachings of Experience* (London, 1869).
Cooper, Thomas, *The Life of Thomas Cooper*, 2d ed. (London, 1872)
Garnett, Richard, *Life of W. J. Fox* (N. Y. and London, 1910).
Holyoake, G. J., *Life of Rev. Joseph Rayner Stephens* (London, 1881).
——, *The Life and Character of Henry Hetherington* (London, 1849).
——, *Sixty Years of an Agitator's Life*, 2 vols. (London, 1900).
Linton, W. J., *Memories* (London, 1895).
Lovett, William, *Life and Struggles of William Lovett in His Pursuit of Bread, Knowledge, and Freedom* (London, 1876).
McCabe, Joseph, *Life and Letters of George Jacob Holyoake*, 2 vols. (London, 1908).
Muirhead, J. H. (Editor), *Nine Famous Birmingham Men* (Birmingham, 1909).
Monypenny, W. F., *Life of Benjamin Disraeli* (London, 1910-   ).
Morley, John, *Life of William Ewart Gladstone*, 3 vols. (London and N. Y., 1903).
Richard, Henry, *Memoirs of Joseph Sturge* (London, 1864).
Solly, Rev. Henry, *These Eighty Years, or The Story of an Unfinished Life*, 2 vols. (London, 1893).
Stanton, Henry B., *Sketches of Reforms and Reformers of Great Britain and Ireland* (N. Y., 1849).
Trevelyan, G. M., *The Life of John Bright* (London, 1913).
Watkins, John, *Life, Poetry and Letters of Ebenezer Elliott, the Corn-Law Rhymer* (London, 1850).

4. *Periodicals*

The Antidote. Ed. by John Brindley (Chester, 1842).
Anti-Socialist Gazette. Ed. by John Brindley (Chester, 1841-1842).
The Beacon, A Weekly Journal of Free Inquiry. Pub. by Henry Hetherington (1844).
Bronterre's National Reformer in Government, Law, Property, Religion and Morals. Ed. by James Bronterre O'Brien (1837).
The Building Societies Record and Provident Man's Manual (1846).

The Champion of What is True and Right and for the Good of All. Ascribed to Richard Oastler but really edited by Rev. J. R. Stephens (1849-1850).

The Christian Investigator, and Evangelical Reformer for the Promotion of Sound Religious Knowledge, and the Inculcation of Temperance and Peace, and the Whole Religion of Christ, vol. i (London, 1862).

Chartist Circular. Published under the supervision of the Universal Central Committee for Scotland. Ed. by William Thompson (Glasgow, 1839-1842).

Cooper's Journal: or, Unfettered Thinker and Plain Speaker for Truth, Freedom, and Progress (1850).

The Commonweal (London, 1845).

The Communist Chronicle and Communist Apostle. Ed. by Goodwyn Barmby.

The Divinearian. Ed. by James E. Duncan. (Commenced in London, 1849).

The English Republic. Ed. by W. J. Linton (London, 1851-1854).

The English Chartist Circular. Ed. by James Harris (London, 1841-42).

The Evangelical Reformer, and Young Man's Guide, vol. i (1838), vol. ii (1839-40). Edited by Joseph Barker (London).

Evenings with the People. Ed. by Ernest Jones (London, 1856).

Fleet Papers. Ed. by Richard Oastler while in the Fleet prison, 1840-44.

The Herald of Redemption. Changed to the *Herald of Coöperation,* beginning with April, 1847. Ed. by James Hole (1847-1848).

Herald of the Future (1839-1840).

The Labourer: A Monthly Magazine of Politics, Literature, Poetry, etc. Ed. by Feargus O'Connor and Ernest Jones (1847-48).

The Life Boat: A Weekly Political Pamphlet. Ed. by William Hill (started in 1843).

The London Chartist Monthly Magazine (started in June, 1843).

The London Democrat. Ed. by George Julian Harney and others (started April 13, 1839).

McDouall's Chartist and Republican Journal. Ed. by P. M. McDouall (Manchester, 1841).

The Model Republic. Published by the Society for the Encouragement of Socialist and Democratic Literature.

The Monthly Circular of the Coöperative League. (Isle of Man and London.)

The Moral Reformer. Ed. by J. Livesey (London, 1838-1839).

The Movement, Anti-Persecution Gazette, and Register of Progress: A Weekly Journal. Ed. by G. J. Holyoake, assisted by M. G. Ryall (1843-1845).

The National: A Library for the People. Ed. by W. J. Linton (London, 1839).

The National Instructor (London, 1850-1851).

The New Age, Concordium Gazette and Temperance Advocate (London, 1843-1844).

Notes to the People. Ed. by Ernest Jones. 2 vols. (1851-1852).

The Oracle of Reason: or Philosophy Vindicated. Ed. by Thomas Paterson, vol. i (London, 1842). Originally edited by Charles Southwell until sentenced to prison, Jan. 15, 1842, for blasphemy.

The People: Their Rights and Liberties, Their Duties and Their Interests. Ed. by Joseph Barker (Wortley, 1849-1852).

The People's Press and Monthly Historical Newspaper. Ed. by William Shirrefs (1847).

The People's Magazine. Ed by J. R. Stephens (Leeds, 1841-1842).

The Political Economist; and Journal of Social Science (1856-1857).

The Power of Pence. Ed. by O'Brien (1848-1849).

The Precursor of Unity. A Monthly Magazine for the Many (started January, 1844).

The Puppet Show (1848).

The Reasoner. Ed. by G. J. Holyoake (1849 *et seq.*).

The Reasoner: and Herald of Progress.

The Reformer. Ed. by Washington Wilkes. No. 1 of the new series appeared Jan., 1846.

The Reformer's Almanac and Companion to the Almanacs, for 1848. Ed. by Joseph Barker.

The Republican: A Magazine Advocating the Sovereignty of the People. Ed. by C. G. Harding (London, 1848).

Reynolds Weekly Newspaper. Ed. by G. W. M. Reynolds.

The Shepherd. Ed. by Rev. J. E. Smith (London, 1834-1837).

The Social Pioneer: or Record of the Progress of Socialism. Ed. by Epicurus (1839).

The Social Reformer. Ed. by J. Bronterre O'Brien and Friends (London, 1849).

The Spirit of the Times; or the Social Reformer. Published by Luke Hansard (London, 1847).

The Standard of Freedom. Published by J. Cassell (London, 1848).

The Ten Hours Advocate and Journal of Literature and Art (1846-1847).

The Truth Teller. Published by B. S. Treanor (Stalybridge, 1848).

The Uxbridge Spirit of Freedom: and Workingman's Vindicator. Conducted by Workingmen (1849).

The Weekly Adviser and Artisan's Companion (Stoke-upon-Trent, 1852).

The Voice of the People. A Supplement to All Newspapers (April 22, 1848, to May 13, 1848).

*The Working-Man's Charter; or the Voice of the People, Advocating
Their Spiritual and Moral Improvement* (London, 1849).
The Working Man's Friend, and Family Instructor.

5. *Pamphlets*

*The Speech of Lord Ashley, M. P., in the House of Commons on Tues-
day, Feb. 28, 1843, on " The Moral and Religious Education of the
Working Classes."* 38 pp. (London, 1843).
Barker, Joseph. Eight bound volumes of pamphlets in the Union The-
ological Seminary Library.
———, *The Gospel Triumphant: or a Defense of Christianity against
the Attacks of the Socialists; and an Exposure of the Infidel
Character and Mischievous Tendency of the Social System of
Robert Owen* (Lancaster, 1839).
Bayley, R. S., *History and Objects of the People's College, Sheffield.*
A Lecture delivered at the Eastern Institution on Thursday eve-
ning, Dec. 18, 1845.
Beard, J. R., *The Religion of Jesus Christ Defended from the Assaults
of English Chartism.* In nine lectures (London. No date).
Brown, George, *An Address to All Classes of Reformers, But Especi-
ally to Those who are Unjustly Excluded from the Franchise.* 16
pp. (Leicester, 1848).
Carlile, Richard, *An Address to that Portion of the People of Great
Britain and Ireland Calling Themselves Reformers, on the Political
Excitement of the Time* (Manchester, 1839).
The Chartist Correspondence (reprinted from the *Free Press*), serial
no. xiii.
Close, Rev. F., *A Sermon Addressed to the Chartists of Cheltenham,
Sunday, August 18, 1839, on the Occasion of Their Attending the
Parish Church in a Body* (London, 1839).
———, *A Sermon Addressed to the Female Chartists of Cheltenham,
Sunday, August 25, 1839, on the Occasion of Their Attending the
Parish Church in a Body* (London, 1839).
*The Contract: Monopolies and Monopolists Tested by the Example of
Jesus Christ by a Member of the Conference of Ministers of Re-
ligion of All Denominations, lately held in Manchester* (London,
1842).
Cooper, Thomas, *Two Orations Against Taking Away Human Life,
under Any Circumstance; and in Explanation, and Defense, of the
Misrepresented Doctrine of Non-Resistance.* 56 pp. (London, 1846).
Craig, E. T., *The Irish Land and Labour Questions Illustrated in the
History of Ralahine and Coöperative Farming* (London, 1882).
DeBary, R. B., *A Charm Against Chartism* (London, 1839).
The Designs of the Chartists, and Their Probable Consequences. A

letter addressed to Mr. James Ibbetson, Bookseller, Bradford.
(Copied from the Leeds *Mercury* of August 3, 1839.) 12 pp.

A Narrative of the Experiences and Sufferings of William Dodd, a Factory Cripple. Written by Himself. 45 pp. (London, 1841).

An Earnest Plea both for the Poor and for the Rich. A Letter to the Right Honourable Sir Robert Peel, Bart., In Which it is Shown How the New Poor-Law Machinery May be Made the Instrument of Diffusing Immediate and Universal Blessings Throughout the Land. By a Parochial Clergyman. 15 pp. (1842).

England and Physical Force Chartism (1838).

A Few Words to the Chartist by a Friend. 16 pp.

A Few Words with Henry Vincent by a Radical Conservative (1840).

Finsbury Lectures. Reports of Lectures Delivered at the Chapel in South Place, Finsbury, by W. J. Fox (London, 1835).

A Friendly Appeal, or Word of Advice, to the Middle and Working Classes of Great Britain, etc. (London, 1839).

Gore, Montague, *A Letter to the Middle Classes on the Present Disturbed State of the Country, Especially with Reference to the Chartist Meetings* (London, 1839).

The Trial of George Jacob Holyoake on an Indictment for Blasphemy. Notes taken by Mr. Hunt (London, 1842).

Hunt, Thomas, *Chartism, Trades Unionism, and Socialism; or, Which is the Best Calculated to Produce Permanent Relief to the Working Classes? A Dialogue.* 20 pp. (London, 1840).

Jenkins, Rev. Evan, *Chartism Unmasked,* 19th ed., Merthyr Tydvil, 1840.

Jones, Ernest, *The Right of Public Meeting: A Letter Addressed (before sentence) to Lord Chief Justice Sir Thomas Wilde* (reprinted in 1887).

A Letter from One of the Special Constables in London on the Late Occasion of their being Called Out to Keep the Peace. 23 pp. (London, 1848).

Jones, William, *Speech on the Charter.* 16 pp.

Larkin, Charles, *A Letter to the Reformers of South Shields on the Elective Franchise.* 20 pp. (Newcastle-upon-Tyne, 1837).

Leach, J., *The Working Man's Arguments in Favor of the Charter.* 8 pp. (Manchester, 1848).

Letters to the Mob by Libertas. 21 pp. (London, 1848).

A Letter to the Radicals and Chartists of Manchester and Lancashire on the Position of the Chartists and Corn-Law Repealers by a Corn-Law Repealer and a Chartist (Manchester, 1840).

Letter from Mr. Lovett to Messrs. Donaldson and Mason. Containing his Reasons for Refusing to be Nominated Secretary of the National Charter Association. 4 pp.

Lovett, William, *Address from the Members of the National Associa-*

tion for Promoting the Political and Social Improvement of the People to the Working Classes of France, on the Subject of War. 2d ed. (London, 1846).

Lovett, William, Cabinet-maker, and John Collins, Tool-maker, *Chartism: A New Organization of the People.* 2d ed. (London, 1841).

——, *Justice Safer than Expediency: An Appeal to the Middle Classes on the Question of the Suffrage* (London, 1848).

——, *Social and Political Morality* (London, 1853).

——, *The Radical Reformers of England, Scotland and Wales to the Irish People. Voted to be written and sent by a meeting of delegates in Palace Yard, London, Sept. 17, 1838.*

The Trial of William Lovett, Journeyman Cabinet-maker, for a Seditious Libel, Before Mr. Justice Littledale, at the Assizes of Warwick, on Tuesday, the 6th of August, 1839. 19pp. (London, 1839).

Speeches Delivered at the Soirée, Held at the National Hall, Holborn, on Wednesday, Feb. 23, 1848, upon the Occasion of the Presentation of a Testimonial to William Lovett. 33 pp.

Manifesto of the General Convention of the Industrious Classes, signed by Hugh Craig, Chairman, and William Lovett, Secretary.

Marshall, Andrew, *The Duty of Attempting to Reconcile the Unenfranchised with the Enfranchised Classes* (Edinburgh, 1841).

Trial of Peter Murry McDouall, Surgeon of Lancashire, and Member of the National Convention from Ashton-under-Lyne, in the Crown Court at the City of Chester, on Friday, the 16th of August, for a Misdemeanor. Before Baron Gurney. Revised and Corrected by Peter Murry McDouall. 64 pp. (1839).

The Members of the Working Man's Association to their Fellow Workers of All Trades. 4 pp.

Memoranda of the Chartist Agitation in Dundee. 80 pp. (Dundee).

Minutes of the Proceedings of the Conference of Representatives of the Middle and Working Classes of Great Britain, Held First at the Waterloo Rooms, and Afterwards at the Town Hall, Birmingham; April 5th, 1842, and Three Following Days. 42 pp. (Birmingham, 1842).

Moral Force: A Reply to an Address Entitled "Physical Force." By a Workingman. 15 pp. (Leicester, 1848).

Morgan, John Minton, *The Christian Commonwealth.*

Metcalf, John James, *Temporal Prosperity Ensured to Mankind by the Practice of Christianity, and Proposals for Establishing a Society to be Entitled, "The Practical Christian Union"* (London).

Munns, Rev. Thomas, *A Letter to the Right Hon. Lord Ashley, on the Condition of the Working Classes in Birmingham, Considered in Reference to Improvement in the Condition of the Same Classes in*

Manufacturing Districts, and Large Towns Generally (Birmingham, 1842).

A Night with the Chartists, Frost, Williams, and Jones. A Narrative of Adventures in Monmouthshire. 15 pp. (London, 1847).

Jones, William, *Speech on the Charter.* 16 pp.

Mr. O'Brien's Vindication. His Defense of the Actions of the Chartists from the Denunciations of O'Connor. 24 pp.

O'Connor, Arthur, *State of Ireland* (London, 1843).

Trial of Feargus O'Connor, Esq., and 58 other Chartists on a Charge of Seditious Conspiracy. Wednesday, March 1, 1843. (Lancaster.)

What May be Done with Three Acres of Land, Explained in the Following Letter by Feargus O'Connor, Esq., M. P.

Pearson, Rev. George, *The Progress and Tendencies of Socialism. A Sermon Preached before the University of Cambridge on Sunday, November 17, 1839* (Cambridge, 1839).

Peel, Frank, *The Risings of the Luddites, Chartists and Plug-Drawers.* 3d ed. (Brighouse, 1895).

Robert Kemp Phelp's Vindication of His Political Conduct and an Explanation of the Misrepresentations of the Northern Star, Together with a Few Words of Advice to Chartists. 28 pp. (Bath).

The People's Charter; an Abstract from " The Rights of Nations" by the Author of "The Rights of Nations," etc. 2d ed. (London, 1832).

The People's Charter and Old England Forever (London, 1839).

Political Monopoly Hostile to the Spirit and Progress of Christianity. By a Norwich Operative. 12 pp.

The Question, "What is a Chartist?" Answered. By the Finsbury Tract Society.

The Real Chartist; Patriotically Addressed to the Consideration of All Republicans, Chartists, Reformers, Radicals, Whigs, Tories, and Conservatives by C. L., a Working Man. 4th ed. (London, 1848).

Report of the Conference of Ministers of All Denominations on the Corn Laws Held in Manchester, August 17th-20th, 1841, With a Digest of the Documents Contributed during the Conference (London, 1841).

The Rise and Fall of Chartism in Monmouthshire. 90 pp.

Reflections upon the Past Policy and Future Prospects of the Chartist Party. Also, A Letter Condemnatory of Private Assassination, as Recommended by Mr. G. J. Harney. By Thomas Clark, Provisional Secretary to the National Charter Association. 16 pp. (1850).

The Rejected Letters. By William Hill. 8 pp. (1843).

Rowlings, J., *Animadversions upon a Sermon Preached by Mr. John Warburton, Minister of the Gospel at Zion Chapel, Union Street, Trowbridge, Sunday Morning, May 26, 1839, upon the Doctrine of Non-Resistance to the Higher Powers.* 23 pp.

Rules and Regulations of the General Convention of the Industrious Classes. 12 pp. (1840).

Short Review of the Political Events of the Past Year, as Contained in the Second Annual Report of the Glasgow Conservative Operatives' Association. Read at the Annual Meeting, on Tuesday Evening, January 29, 1839 (Glasgow, 1839).

Slaney, Robert A., *Reports of the House of Commons on the Education (1838) and on the Health (1840) of the Poorer Classes in Large Towns, with Some Suggestions for Improvement* (London, 1841).

Socialism. A Commentary on the Public Discussion on the Subjects of Necessity and Responsibility, between M. A. Campbell, Social Missionary, and the Rev. J. T. Bannister, of Coventry. By Jonathan Jonathan, late of the United States. 42 pp. (Coventry, 1839).

Lectures Against Socialism. Delivered under the Direction of the Committee of the London City Missions (London, 1840).

Spencer, Thomas, *The Pillars of the Church of England* (1840).

———, *Religion and Politics* (1840).

———, *Practical Suggestions on Church Reform* (1840).

———, *Clerical Conformity and Church Property* (1840).

———, *The Prayer Book Opposed to the Corn Laws* (1841).

———, *Want of Fidelity of Ministers of Religion Respecting the New Poor Law,* four parts (1841).

———, *The Reformed Prayer Book of 1842* (1842).

———, *The Second Reformation* (1842).

———, *The People's Rights and How to Get Them* (1843).

State of the Question between the People, the Middle Classes and the Aristocracy. By a Member of the Northern Political Union. 24 pp. (Newcastle-upon-Tyne, 1839).

Stephens, J. R., *A Sermon Delivered at Hyde, in Lancashire, on Sunday Evening Last, February 17, 1839.*

———, *Sermon Preached on Shepherd and Shepherdess Fields* (London, 1839).

———, *Sermon on Primrose Hill* (1839).

———, *Sermon on Kennington Common* (1839).

———, *A Sermon Preached in his Chapel at Charlestown on Sunday, January 6, 1839, Being the First Sabbath After His Release from the New Bailey at Manchester* (London).

———, *The Political Christian Pulpit.*

Stowell, Rev. Hugh, *A Plea for the Working-Man: Do Not Lower His Wages: Adressed to Employers.* 8 pp. (Manchester, 1848).

———, *No Revolution. A Word to the People of England.* 3d ed., 7 pp. (Manchester, 1848).

Is There Not One Law for the Rich and Another for the Poor? Being a Reply by a Workingman to the " No Revolution," Lately Published by the Rev. Hugh Stowell. 8 pp. (Manchester, 1848).

Trevelyan, Arthur, *To the People: Moral Lunacy or Our Class Legislators, and Their Supporters, Demonstrated* (London, 1849).

The True Briton of the Nineteenth Century: Government Aids of Chartism, Socialism, and Popery. 16 pp. (London, 1840).

A Voice from the Millions. By a Norwich Operative. 4th ed., 20 pp.

A Word to the Masses on Their Right to the Franchise, and the Means of Attaining It. By a Norwich Operative. 2d ed., 16 pp.

Watkins, John, *The Five Cardinal Points of the People's Charter Separately Explained and Advocated.* 15 pp.

———, *Impeachment of Feargus O'Connor* (London, 1843).

———, *Lovettism vs. Chartism. A Chartist Sermon.*

Whiggery, Chartism, and Truth. Being an Exposure of the Whigs. A Reply to the Misstatement of the Sunderland Herald, and a Defense of the Chartists (Sunderland, 1839).

White, John, *England and Her Interests; the " Times " and the Government and the Anti-Corn Law League Considered* (London, 1843).

Whittaker, J. W., *A Sermon Preached at the Parish Church, Blackburn, on Sunday, August 4, 1839.* 18 pp. (Blackburn, 1839).

CHARTISM IN THE REVIEWS

Blackwood's Magazine, vol. xxvi, pp. 289 *et seq.* (Sept. 1839), and vol. lxiii, p. 660 (May, 1848).

Contemporary Review, article on Gerald Massey, in May, 1904.

Edinburgh Review, vol. 95, pp. 240 *et seq.*, and vol. 88, pp. 375 *et seq.*

Gentleman's Magazine, vol. xii, p. 301.

THE CHURCHES

THE CHURCH OF ENGLAND AND THE CATHOLIC CHURCH

1. *History*

Balleine, G. R., *A History of the Evangelical Party* (London, 1908).

Church, R. W., *The Oxford Movement* (London, 1897).

Cornish, F. W., *The English Church in the Nineteenth Century.* 2 vols. (London, 1910).

Legg, J. Wickham, *English Church Life from the Restoration to the Tractarian Movement* (London, 1914).

MacCaffrey, Rev. James, *History of the Catholic Church in the Nineteenth Century.* 2 vols. (Dublin, 1909).

McCarthy, Michael, *Church and State in England and Wales* (London, 1906).

Overton, J. H., *The Anglican Revival* (Chicago and N. Y., 1898).
———, *The Church in England*. 2 vols. (London, 1897).
Palmer, William, *A Narrative of Events Connected with the Publication of the Tracts for the Times* (London, 1883).
Patterson, Rev. M. W., *A History of the Church of England* (London, 1909).
Perry, G. G., *A History of the English Church. Third Period* (London, 1890).
Rogers, J. G., *The Church Systems of England in the Nineteenth Century* (London, 1881).
Spence, Very Rev. H. D. M., *The Church of England*. 4 vols. (London, 1897-98).
Thureau-Dangin, Paul, *The English Catholic Revival in the Nineteenth Century*. 2 vols. (London, 1914).

2. Biography

Abbott, Edwin A., *The Anglican Career of Cardinal Newman* (London, 1892).
Arnold, Frederick, *Robertson of Brighton* (London, 1886).
Bloomfield, Alfred, *A Memoir of Charles James Bloomfield, D. D., Bishop of London, with Selections from His Correspondence*. 2 vols. (London, 1863).
Brooke, Stopford A., *Life and Letters of Frederick W. Robertson, M. A., Incumbent of Trinity Chapel, Brighton, 1847-53*. 2 vols. (London, 1865). One vol. ed. (N. Y., no date).
Denison, George Anthony, *Notes of My Life, 1805-1878*. 3d ed. (London, 1879).
Fitzpatrick, W. J., *Memoirs of Richard Whately*. 2 vols. (London, 1864).
Guiney, Louise I., *Hurrell Froude, Memoranda and Comments* (London, 1904).
Hare, Augustus J. C., *The Story of My Life*. 2 vols. (N. Y., 1896).
Hutton, W. H., *Letters of William Stubbs* (London, 1904).
Kaufmann, M., *Charles Kingsley* (London, 1892).
Charles Kingsley: His Letters and Memories of His Life. Edited by His Wife. 10th ed., 2 vols. (London, 1878).
Liddon, H. P., *Life of Edward B. Pusey*, 4 vols. (London, 1893).
Lock, Walter, *John Keble*. 3d ed. (London, 1893).
Maurice, Frederick, *The Life of Frederick Denison Maurice Chiefly Told in His Own Letters*. 2 vols. (N. Y., 1884).
Mozley, Anne (editor), *Letters and Correspondence of John Henry Newman during His Life in the English Church* (London, 1890).
Mozley, Rev. T., *Reminiscences Chiefly of Oriel College and the Oxford Movement*. 2 vols. (London, 1882).

Newman, J. H., *Apologia Pro Vita Sua* (London, 1864; Everyman's edition, 1913).

Overton, J. H., and Elizabeth Wordsworth, *Christopher Wordsworth, Bishop of London, 1807-1885* (London, 1888).

Pattison, Mark, *Memoirs* (London, 1885).

Purcell, E. S., *Life of Cardinal Manning, Archbishop of Westminster.* 2 vols. (N. Y., 1896).

Stephens, W. R. W., *The Life and Letters of Walter F. Hook, D. D.* 2 vols. (London, 1880).

Stanley, A. P., *Addresses and Charges of Edward Stanley, with a Memoir* (London, 1852).

Ward, Wilfred, *The Life of John Henry Cardinal Newman.* 2 vols. (London and N. Y., 1913).

——, *William George Ward and the Catholic Revival* (London, 1893).

——, *William George Ward and the Oxford Movement* (London, 1890).

Wordsworth, Charles, *Annals of My Life.* 2 vols. (London, 1891, 1893).

Whately, E. Jane, *Life and Correspondence of Richard Whately, D. D., Late Archbishop of Dublin.* 2 vols. (London, 1866).

3. Church of England Periodicals

British Critic.
The English Review.
The Christian Guardian and Church of England Magazine.
The Christian Remembrancer: A Monthly Magazine and Review.
The Christian Observer.
The Church of England Magazine.
Quarterly Review.

Tracts for the Times. Especially No. 86

THE METHODIST CHURCH

1. History

A New History of Methodism. Edited by W. J. Townshend, H. B. Workman and George Ayres. 2 vols. (London, 1909).

The Jubilee of the Methodist New Connexion. By Thomas Allen, William Cooke, Samuel Hulme and Philip James Wright (London, 1848).

Baxter, M., *Memorials of the United Methodist Free Churches, With Recollections of the Rev. Robert Eckett and Some of His Contemporaries* (1865).

Gregory, Benjamin, *Sidelights on the Conflicts of Methodism during the Second Quarter of the Nineteenth Century, 1827-1852* (London, 1898).

Hurst, J. F., *History of Methodism.* 7 vols. (N. Y., 1902-04). Volumes I to III on British Methodism are written by T. E. Brigden.

Methodism as It Is, With Some of its Antecedents, its Branches and Disruptions; Including a Diary of the Campaign of 1849, Protracted during a Period of Seven Years; With Special Reference to the Character, Power, Policy and Administration of the " Master Mind " of John Wesley's Legislative Succession. Published anonymously but written by James Everett. 2 vols. (London, 1863-1865).

North, E. M., *Early Methodist Philanthropy* (N. Y., 1914).

Petty, John, *The History of the Primitive Methodist Connexion.* New ed. (London, 1880).

Smith, George, *History of Wesleyan Methodism.* 3 vols. (London, 1861).

Stevens, Abel, *History of Methodism.* 3 vols. (1858-1861).

2. Polity

Gregory, Benj., *A Handbook of Scriptural Church Principles and Wesleyan Methodist Polity and History* (London, 1888).

Kendall, H. B., *Handbook of Primitive Methodist Church Principles, History and Polity* (London, 1905).

Pierce, William, *The Ecclesiastical Principles and Polity of the Wesleyan Methodists.* 3d ed. (London, 1873).

Rigg, J. H., *The Connexional Economy of Wesleyan Methodism in its Ecclesiastical and Spiritual Aspects* (London, 1879).

Skewes, J. H., *A Complete and Popular Digest of the Polity of Methodism* (London, 1869).

Wansborough, Charles E., *Handbook and Index to the Minutes of the Conference: Showing the Growth and Development of the Wesleyan Methodist Constitution from the First Conference, 1744, to 1890* (London, 1890).

Watson, Richard, *An Affectionate Address.*

Williams, H. W., *The Constitution and Polity of Wesleyan Methodism* (London, 1880).

3. Biography

Avery, John G., *Memorials of the Rev. John Henley* (London, 1844).

Beaumont, Joseph, *The Life of the Rev. Joseph Beaumont, M. D.* (London, 1856).

Beech, John H., *The Good Soldier* (London, 1856).

Bunting, T. P., *The Life of Jabez Bunting, D. D.* 2 vols. (London, 1859, 1887).

Chew, Richard, *James Everett: A Biography* (London, 1875).

Dixon, R. W., *Life of James Dixon, D. D.* (London, 1874).

Davison, John, *Life of the Venerable William Clowes* (London, 1854).

Faulkner, J. Alfred, *The Socialism of John Wesley*, in *"Social Tracts for the Times."* 24 pp. (London, no date).

Memoirs of Rev. Joseph Entwisle by His Son (London, 1854).

Everett, James, *Memoirs of the Life, Character and Ministry of William Dawson* (Philadelphia, 1843).

———, *Wesleyan Takings, Centenary Sketches of Ministerial Character.* Published anonymously (1841).

Jackson, Thomas, *Recollections of My Own Life and Times* (London, 1873).

Jobson, Frederick J., *A Tribute to the Memory of Rev. Jabez Bunting, D. D.* (London, 1858).

———, *The Beloved Disciple: A Sermon Preached in Wesley Chapel, Lincoln, Jan. 26, 1868, on the Death of Rev. John Hannah, D. D., With a Biographical Sketch of the Deceased* (London, 1868).

Macdonald, Frederic W., *The Life of William Morley Punshon.* 3d ed. (London, 1888).

M'Cullagh, T. M., *The Earnest Life: Memorials of the Rev. Thomas Keysell* (London, 1867).

M'Owan, John, *A Man of God; or, Providence and Grace Exemplified in a Memoir of the Rev. Peter M'Owan* (London, 1873).

4. Magazines

The Wesleyan Methodist Magazine.
The Wesleyan Association Magazine.
The Methodist New Connexion Magazine.
The Primitive Methodist Magazine.
The Wesleyan Vindicator. Published during the crisis of 1849.

The Minutes of the Wesleyan Methodist Conference.

The Other Nonconformist Churches

Carlile, J. C., *The Story of the English Baptists* (London, 1905).

Dale, R. W., *History of English Congregationalism* (N. Y. and London, 1907).

Book of Christian Discipline of the Religious Society of Friends in Great Britain (London, 1883).

Epistles from the Yearly Meeting of Friends, Held in London, to the Quarterly and Monthly Meetings in Great Britain, Ireland, and Elsewhere; from 1681 to 1857, Inclusive: With an Historical Introduction, and a Chapter Comprising Some of the Early Epistles and Records of the Yearly Meetings. 2 vols. (London, 1858).

Emmott, Elizabeth B., *The Story of Quakerism* (London, 1908).

Miall, Edward, *The British Churches.* 2d ed. (London, 1850).

Stoughton, John, *History of Religion in England.* 8 vols. (London, 1881-84).

Waddington, John, *Congregational History. Continuation to 1850* (London, 1878).

———

Adamson, William, *The Life of Joseph Parker* (London and Edinburgh, 1902).

Arnot, William, *Life of James Hamilton* (London, 1870).

Memoirs of the Life of Elizabeth Fry, with Extracts from Her Letters and Journal. Edited by Two of Her Daughters. 2 vols. (Philadelphia, 1848).

Hood, Edwin P., *The Earnest Minister: A Record of the Life and Selections from Posthumous and Other Writings of the Rev. Benjamin Parsons, of Ebley, Gloucestershire* (London, 1846).

Macleod, Donald, *Memoirs of Norman Macleod* (Toronto, 1876).

Miall, Arthur, *Life of Edward Miall* (London, 1884).

Parker, Joseph, *A Preacher's Life* (London, 1899).

Stoughton, John, *Recollections of a Long Life* (London, 1894).

———

The Eclectic Review.
The Evangelical Magazine.
The Nonconformist.

GENERAL RELIGIOUS THOUGHT

Hall, T. C., *The Social Meaning of Modern Religious Movements in England* (N. Y., 1900).

Tulloch, John, *Movement of Religious Thought in Britain during the Nineteenth Century* (London, 1885).

INDEX

Alton Locke, 20, 79
Anti-Corn Law Agitation, 30, 40, 85, 103
Anti-Corn Law Conference, 25, 98

Baptists, 45, 100
Barker, Joseph, 19, 28, 33, 51, 62, 63, 95, 105, 106, 107, 111, 115
Binns, George, 104
Brewster, Rev. Patrick, 18, 107, 111, 112, 114, 118
Bright, John, 104
Broad Church Movement, 75, 80
Bronterre's National Reformer, 34
Bunting, Rev. Jabez, 83, 85, 89

Carlile, Richard, 15, 18
Catholic Church, 104
Chartism Unmasked, 60
Chartist Circular, 42, 47, 49
Chartist Teetotal Societies, 54, 55, 131
Christian Chartist Churches, 22, 27, 42, 102, 108
Christian Guardian and Church of England Magazine, 65
Christian Observer, 38, 67
Christian Remembrancer, 66
Christian Socialists, 80
Church of England Magazine, 13, 67
Cleave, John, 47, 48, 54
Complete Suffrage, 22, 96, 101, 115, 121
Congregational Church, 24, 98
Congregational Magazine, 98
Coningsby, 72
Cooper's Journal, 33
Cooper, Thomas, 16, 18, 33, 51, 55, 95, 101, 102
Cooper, Walter, 15, 18
Convention of 1851, 34, 56

Disraeli, Benjamin, 72

Eclectic Review, 99, 116
Education, 46
Elliott, Ebenezer, 30
Engels, Frederick, 12, 15
The English Chartist Circular, 54
Established Church, 11, 26, 28, 58, 62, 87, 126
Established Church of Scotland, 107

Female Chartist Societies, 56
Fox, W. J., 19, 51, 106, 111
Frost, John, 41

Giles, Rev. Eustace, 10, 18, 28, 113
Griffeth, Rev. William, 83, 91

Hetherington, Henry, 15, 47, 50, 54
Hill, Rev. William, 26, 28, 35, 111, 113
Holyoake, G. J., 15, 18, 76

Jackson, Rev. William, 101, 114
Jenkinson, Rev. John, 101, 112

Kingsley, Rev. Charles, 15, 68, 75, 133

London Working Men's Association, 9, 53, 56, 80
Lovett, William, 19, 33, 46-54, 57

Manchester Conference of Ministers, 107
Maurice, Rev. F. D., 15, 75-79
Methodist New Connexion, 82, 90, 95, 106
Miall, Rev. Edward, 13, 18, 22, 98, 99, 112, 113, 116-118
Militarism, 56
National Complete Suffrage Union, 99
New Poor Law, 10, 94